Killing Me Softly

America's Hidden Agenda
for the Black Community

M. Todd Rawlings

To all of the people in my life
who have carried me through difficult times

CONTENTS

ACKNOWLEDGMENTS

They tell a story of a person who sees two sets of footprints in the sands of his life. During the difficult times, he sees only one set of footprints. The Lord tells him that, during those times, He carried the man.

My life has not been like that.

For me, I can see three sets of footprints. During difficult times, there would be two. There would be two sets of footprints because, during those tough times, there has always been a friend or family member to carry me. The second set is the Lord Who gave them strength.

The Lord tells US to bear one another's burdens. So, I bear a deep sense of gratitude for all the people in my life who have carried me until I could walk again by myself.

"Bear one another's burdens,
and thereby fulfill the law of Christ."
— Galatians 6:2

CHAPTER I
Whose Life Matters?

"That's asking a lot. You're saying you want a poison, a virus or something, that can differentiate between various groups of people?"

"Yes, and we need to make sure there's a vaccine just in case. We'll need to find or set up a lab in another part of the world. Funding won't be a problem."

"Well, I think there is a lab that would be perfect for such a thing. It is in China, a city called Wuhan."

Six years later:

"So what's the update? Have we gotten any closer? We really need something big."

"We're still very far away. Still, we have a strain that is very contagious. It's not fatal to everyone but to many. It's passed on the same way someone would pass on the flu. There are many precautions that, if taken, could drastically reduce the chances of a person getting it; however, the thing that makes it so promising is this – We already have a cure. Will that work for now?"

"I'll be in touch"

Click.

The Coronavirus first broke out in Wuhan, China. According to reports, it was very contagious and often fatal. It was most deadly on the elderly and those with other ailments. It was the perfect weapon to use in a nursing home to reduce the number of the elderly of whom so many were a drain to the economy in a city like New York.

In New York, people were confined to nursing homes. Ten thousand elderly people marched into buildings where there was no way out. They marched into buildings whose workers told them they would be safe.

They died there.

The prison population was also a targeted group. Many people who are incarcerated provide a tremendous drag on the economy. Those currently in prison cost taxpayers $81B a year. Prisons provide a perfect environment for a weapon like Covid 19.

There was one huge problem though.

Prisons also provide some sort of protection. If the virus never got inside the locked doors, no one would ever catch it, let alone die from it. It was difficult to keep out but, to be effective, there needed to be a way to spread the virus quickly. Unless there was some way to bring it inside in large numbers most of the prison population would survive. If only there was a way to let large numbers of inmates out for a period of time, and then bring them back.

"So, there are groups of people that need to be…well, let's just say their numbers need to be thinned out."

The entire infrastructure of our country is in danger. Our current debt is $25T dollars. Once it hits $30T, it will cost us $1T each year just to service the debt. We collect $3.3T each year in taxes. So, virtually every dime for the first four months of the year will go to our debt payments. We won't have money to run the country until May 1st.

"Let's start with the elderly. They are not productive. They are well past their income producing age. Healthcare alone for them is astronomical. They don't spend money like others, thus don't help the economy.

"Next prisoners. They do very little to help the expansion of America. They produce very little. They have no income, so they pay no taxes. We don't see them at the mall or eating at a restaurant. In

the meantime, we put $81B per year into supporting them. They are a drain on the healthcare system and their very existence is a drag on real estate surrounding prisons."

"But there is one more group. This one is a little trickier. They're spread out. We can't lock them inside somewhere. Most are strong and healthy. You know who I'm talking about? They make up only 6.5% of the country yet commit 51% of all violent crimes. Ninety percent of their families do not have a father in the home. Because of this 45% of the nation's budget goes to welfare, housing, food stamps, etc.

"Do you get it now? It's the group Hillary Clinton called super predators.

"Joe Biden said, 'We have predators on our streets that society has in fact, in part because of its neglect, created. They are beyond the pale many of those people, beyond the pale. And it's a sad commentary on society. **We have no choice but to take them out of society.'**

"Biden described a 'cadre of young people, tens of thousands of them, born out of wedlock, without parents, without supervision, without any structure, without any conscience developing because they literally ... because they literally have not been socialized, they literally have not had an opportunity.'

"We should focus on them now because 'if we don't, they will, or a portion of them, will become the predators 15 years from now.'

"Biden added that he didn't care 'why someone is a malefactor in society' and that criminals needed to be cordoned off from the rest of society, "away from my mother, your husband, our families,' he insisted."

"Wait a minute. Are you actually talking about black people?"

"Absolutely not! We won't target all blacks. Most are tremendously productive. Most are extremely intelligent. Most earn a living. Most pay taxes. Most are a joy to be around. We want to protect them."

"There is a subset, however," his speech tells us, "that we need to, again, 'thin out'. And, besides, it's not just black people in this group. They are black, white, Hispanic, Asian. Yes, it is true, most of them are black."

"I'm sorry. I just don't quite understand. It sounds like you are

specifically talking about black people."

"No, there is black person after black person who is brilliant. There are vast numbers in the population who are educated. They are extremely hard-working people. They are married and have great families. They are highly educated. They make amazing contributions to society.

"But notice my figures. Blacks make up 13.5% of the country. This group is 6.5%. This group commits 51% of violent crimes.

"But, of the 13.5%, at least half never break the law, let alone kill someone. The percentage of black households without a father living with the family is 75%. Yet there are 90% of this group living without a father."

"The reality is that there are two groups of black people in this country. One group contributes, creates, and is productive. This other group, super predators as Hillary said, is a tremendous cost and burden. To 'thin them out' could change this country.

"Besides, it isn't like we haven't done it before."

Note: The number of black people in the US who have caught COVID in comparison to the number of white, non-Hispanic people in the community is 2.6 times higher.

The number of black people in the US who have been hospitalized due to COVID in comparison to the number of white, non-Hispanic people in the community is 4.6 times higher.

The number of black people in the US who have died of COVID in comparison to the number of white, non-Hispanic people in the community is 2.1 times higher.

The attempted explanation of the disparity in these numbers is the high number of black people with other illnesses. This argument falls apart when one considers the fact that the mortality rate in the US of black Americans is 75 years old and that of white Americans is 78.6. These numbers simply do not support black American's cases being almost 3 times that of the white population and hospitalizations almost 5 times that of the white population.

Let that sink in. The black community is dying of COVID at over twice the rate of the white community. Why?

The second argument is the proximity of the black community to each other in big cities.

Those holding this claim, however, do not figure this into the deaths in the US compared to other countries. They like to tout the number of deaths in the US to other countries yet do not consider the sheer number of Americans who live in proximity to each other. It is a mere statistic of convenience.

If one believes the statistics from other countries, we do not see a disproportionate number of deaths coming from Tokyo, New Delhi, or Shanghai. Also, 23 of the top 50 populated cities in the world are in either China or India. We don't see these countries reporting a disproportionate number of cases, hospitalizations, or deaths from COVID. So, once again, why are the numbers of the black community so much higher in these areas than that of the white community?

In contrast, as of this writing, the number of Congressmen and Congresswomen in the US who have died from COVID is 0. The number of Senators in the US who have died of COVID is 0. The number of White House officials who have died of COVID is 0.

In our 50 states, the number of governors who have died of COVID is 0. The number of Attorney Generals who have died of COVID is 0. The number of Lieutenant Governors in the US who have died of COVID is 0.

This number is much harder to obtain, but all indications are that the number of family members of all of these individuals who have died of COVID is...0.

CHAPTER II
When Losing the Battle
May Lose the War

"How are we ever going to promote this woman?" Mark asks. "I mean, she is passionate. She is attractive. She is hard working. On the other hand, she isn't always 'on top of things,' if you know what I mean.

"She has no business experience. She has never held an office. Come on. She has never even managed a 7-11. She'll be eaten alive.

"We need her to relentlessly attack a man who is a best-selling author, the creator of an award-winning TV show, and, oh yeah, a billionaire. Every day, she needs to get people to believe she knows more than he does.

"I don't even believe that. The biggest business decision she ever did was figure out how to make change for a twenty.

"Let's face it. She thinks she knows everything, and she's really not very bright."

Bob thinks hard for a minute.

"Well, what if we have her play the race card?" he asks. "If she says something stupid and someone calls her on it, we can have her call them a racist."

"That's great," Mark says, "except for one thing — she ain't black, Bob."

Bob grimaces.

"As a matter of fact," Mark goes on, "if we stick to the fact there are only three races, she is Caucasian. Even if we accept there are five races, she is still a spoiled little white girl."

"Remember," Bob says, "definitions change as needed. We just need to, once again, revive the term 'people of color'. She will be a 'woman of color'. When someone questions her, they will only be doing it because she is a 'woman of color'. We will convince people she was oppressed her whole life by wicked white guys.

"If she says 2 + 2 = 7 and someone questions her, play the card…racists!

"We change the whole narrative. There are no longer white, black, and Asian people. There are now three races: white, Asian, and 'people of color.' It will no longer be a struggle for equality for black people. It will be a struggle of equality for anyone short of a dark tan."

"I don't know, Bob," Mark says, "It seems to me that will hurt black people more than help. It will set their struggle back years and years.

"I mean, look what they have been through. It seems to me that having 'privileged Latino girls' who both white and black men have showered with love, who grew up in some of the utmost best neighborhoods in the country, who have been given the best parts and the best jobs, suddenly become a persecuted minority, and that would hurt the cause of black people.

"I mean, I'm for anything that helps us, but who in this country has had it worse than a black woman? For a Latino to stand beside a black woman and claim they have shared the same struggles seems an insult. How do you think blacks will respond to that?"

"You're kidding right?" Bob says. "They will respond like they always do. They will help us. They will do what we tell them to do. That's how they will respond."

Alexandria Ocasio-Cortez referred once to the "three branches of Congress." Then, she tried to correct herself and say "the three branches of government – the House, the Senate, and the Presidency." She has mentioned the need to do away with all fossil fuels within 12 years, and we shouldn't worry about the $91T it will cost. She has stated that the world will come to an end in 12 years. She declared that there is no longer an upper middle class. She said that unemployment is low because people are working two jobs. She was excited that Amazon was not going to get a tax credit because now they could spend that money on something else.

When she was challenged on each of these statements, she claimed that they challenged her because she is a "woman of color."

I mean, that must be the reason. What other reason could there be?

Who has had a more difficult struggle than black women?

In their homes, 75% have no father living there. Black men often prefer white women, Asian women, or Latino women.

There are lazy white people. There are lazy Hispanics. Yes, there are lazy black people.

I am going to cross the line this one time, however, and make a generalization. Black women are not lazy! They are very intelligent. They are persistent. They are beautiful. I have nothing but respect for them. The obstacles they have had to surmount are so much larger than any other group of people in our society. To take other women whose skin is somewhat darker than a white person's and group them with these beautiful women as if they have any idea what they have gone through is insulting and cruel.

It implies that these other "women of color" can somehow relate to a black woman's struggles. It implies that other "women of color" have accomplished as much as a successful black woman has.

They rarely have.

Whatever other opinions I have, whatever beliefs I may have, there is one thing I am sure of. Few people deserve more respect than black women.

Today the term **"person of color"** is primarily used to

describe any person who is not considered to be white in the United States. During various periods in US history, persons of color included African Americans, Latino Americans, Italian Americans, Asian Americans, Native Americans, Pacific Islander Americans, Middle Eastern Americans, and multiracial Americans.

The term "colored" was originally equivalent to the term "person of color", but usage of the term "colored" gradually came to be restricted to "negroes", and it is now considered a racial slur. Yet, for some reason, "people of color" isn't offensive if the right people use it.

The term "people of color" was initially used to refer to light-skinned people of mixed African and European heritage. The term was used to distinguish between slaves who were "mostly black" or "negro" and free people who were primarily "mixed race." After the American Civil War, however, "colored" was used as a label exclusively for black Americans.

Martin Luther King, Jr. used the term "citizens of color" in 1963. Since then, its meaning has changed radically. The term "person of color" is really just an equivalent for the condescending term "non-white."

The phrase "women of color" was developed and introduced for widespread use by a group of black women activists at the National Women's Conference in 1977.

According to Stephen Satris of Clemson University, in the United States, there are two main racial divides. The first is the "black-white" delineation; the second is the delineation "between whites and everyone else," with "whites" being "narrowly construed" and "everyone else" being called "people of color."

You may wonder why I have made such a big deal of this.

It is because making the struggles of other ethnic groups equal to those of blacks in the US is preposterous. It is especially preposterous when it comes to black women and all other "women of color." Whatever offenses that have been made against other groups has to take into account the unique experiences of black people. Latinos may have causes for complaints, but "Latino" is an ethnic group and NOT a race.

Fast forward:

In politics today we have what has been called "The Squad." Let's take a test. Without looking it up, could you name the four squad members?

Quick. Write them down.

____

____

____

____

How did you do? Some of you got all four. Some got two. Here they are:

IIhan Omar
Alexandria Ocasio Cortez
Rashida Tliab
Ayanna Pressley

I would wager to guess that the one person that was remembered the least was Ayanna Presley.
That is a real shame.

This is from the site "Meet Ayanna:"

Like many in her district, Congresswoman Pressley has

endured numerous hardships throughout her life, and it is because of those experiences that she remains a dedicated activist who's devoted to creating robust and informed policies that speak to the intersectionality of her district's lived experiences. She believes that the people closest to the pain should be closest to the power and that a diversity of voices in the political process is essential to making policies that benefit more Americans.

Born in Cincinnati and raised in Chicago, Congresswoman Pressley is the only child of a single mother and a father who was in and out of the criminal justice system - creating an unstable household and forcing her to mature at a rapid rate. While her father ultimately overcame his addiction and went on to become a published author, Congresswoman Pressley was primarily raised by her mother Sandra Pressley, a tenants' rights organizer who instilled in her the value of civic engagement. Thanks to her mother's dedication to activism, Congresswoman Pressley has always been acutely aware of the role that government can play in lifting up families and communities.

Congresswoman Pressley attended the Francis W. Parker School, a private school in Chicago where her activism and commitment to public service took hold. A devoted student, Congresswoman Pressley was supported by her teachers, faculty, and peers and was elected class president every year from 7th grade through senior year of high school. She was also elected student government president, was a competitive debater through her school's chapter of Junior State of America, was the commencement speaker for her graduating class, and was named 'most likely to be mayor of Chicago.'

Congresswoman Pressley moved to Boston, MA in 1992 to attend Boston University, however, after a couple of years of enrollment, she withdrew from the University to help support her mother. She remained an activist in the community, working as a senior aide to Congressman Joseph P. Kennedy II, volunteering for Senator John Kerry's reelection campaign, and working for Senator Kerry for 13 years in a variety of roles, including constituency director and political director. Senator Kerry described Congresswoman Pressley as a "force" who "believed in public service."

In 2009, she launched a historic at-large campaign for Boston City Council and won, becoming the first woman of color elected to the Council in its 100-year history. On the Council, Congresswoman Pressley worked in partnership with residents, advocates, and other elected officials to combat the inequities and disparities facing the community. In her eight-year tenure on the Council, she:

• Revised and mandated enforcement of a pregnant and parenting teen policy for Boston Public Schools to strengthen pathways to graduation and to reduce the dropout rate,
• Developed a comprehensive, culturally competent, medically accurate, and age appropriate sexual education and health curriculum, which was successfully adopted as a permanent part of the Boston Public Schools' wellness policy,
• Convened the first "listening-only hearing" in the Boston City Council's history, where 300 families impacted by gun violence and trauma shared their stories with city officials,
• Partnered with the National Black Women's Justice Institute, to develop evidence-based research to reform school disciplinary policies that contribute to the school to prison pipeline for black and Latinx girls, and
• Successfully pushed for the creation of 75 new liquor licenses, 80% dedicated to disenfranchised neighborhoods,

*resulting in the creation of dozens of new restaurants and
hundreds of jobs in local Boston communities.*

*In 2016, Congresswoman Pressley was named one of The
New York Times 14 Young Democrats to Watch. In
2014, the Greater Boston Chamber of Commerce named
her as one of their Ten Outstanding Young Leaders, and
the Victim Rights Law Center presented her with their
Leadership Award. In 2015, she earned the EMILY's
List Rising Star Award and was named one of Boston
Magazine's 50 Most Powerful People. She is also an
Aspen-Rodel Fellow in Public Leadership, Class of
2012.*

I would guess, with all of the press "The Squad" has gotten,
most people didn't know these things about her. I myself
differ with her on many issues but, regardless of anybody's
political opinion, she is an impressive woman.

But, despite her apparent lack of difficulty getting
through life, they need her for a specific reason.

They need her so that anyone challenging them will be
considered to be racists. She rarely makes it to the podium.
She rarely is quoted. But, without her, the squad loses its
legitimacy.

The other three 'white' women can't really pull that off,
can they?

They can now come, arm in arm, as "women of color":
abused, neglected, and forgotten, all the same, by white
men.

They have all lived a horrible life of racism. They have
been held back. None have had the opportunities privileged
white women have had. They are united; they all know the
pain of racism. They are "women of color."

Really? Because I think it is appalling.

To the black community, I ask: How did you let this
happen? How did you fall for this? Shame on you. Shame
on you!!

If and when society asks what you want, you're your demands or wishes are met, please remember black women. They always seem to be forgotten.

Be specific. Don't settle for a bunch of stuff for all "women of color."

Some things fit for all of these groups for sure. But honor black women specifically.

And please stop letting "women of color" degrade and insult black women as if they know exactly what a black woman has endured.

Note: I feel as though I need to say something more about Congresswoman Alexandria Ocasio-Cortez because I have used her as an example to make a point.

I have a lot of respect for this young woman. Her energy and drive have gotten her where she is today. Yes, she has made some remarks that weren't the best. But who among us has not? Who, when thrown into the limelight for the first time, with question after question thrown at them, would not make a mistake?

I have made plenty. I continue to pioneer new mistakes.

Our opinions would be far from each other, but she has been an inspiration to people that their dreams can come true.

Good for this young lady. I wish her nothing but health, safety, and prosperity.

Keep chasing your dreams, Congresswoman. Keep chasing your dreams.

CHAPTER III
That Damn Wall

"Let me get this straight," Mark says, "the idea on the table is that we abandon our position on securing our borders? We oppose the building of structures that we have fought hard to build in the past?"

"That's it," says Bob. "You got it."

"But we have always stood our ground firmly on the idea that people coming into this country illegally are bad for our country. For years we have stood solidly with black Americans on the issue. The more illegal immigrants come in, the fewer jobs for Americans, especially black Americans."

"Yes," Bob agrees, "but that no longer works for us. This will give us a great opportunity to paint the opposition as racists. We need to, once again, play the race card here."

"Ok, help me." Mark is holding his head because it hurts now. "He is against the hundreds of thousands of people coming into our country, like we have always been, because even murderers and rapists running from the law may come with the good people. How then do we make that about race? How does opposition to thousands of people coming across our borders, none them black, make someone a racist?"

*"Come on, Mark, think! They are '***brown*** people'. We stand up for **brown** people."*

"Ok, but part of our stance has always been that it hurts the black community. Larger numbers of people coming in

disproportionately hurt our black communities. We have always stood on the notion that we need to battle illegal immigration because of the negative affects on our black communities. They are already hurting and in need of jobs. How will they respond?"

"You're kidding right? They will respond like they always do. They will help us. That's how they will respond."

To those of the white race who look to the incoming of those of foreign birth and strange tongue and habits for the prosperity of the South, were I permitted I would repeat what I say to my own race, 'Cast down your bucket where you are.' Cast it down among the eight millions of Negroes whose habits you know... As we have proved our loyalty to you in the past ... so in the future, in our humble way, we shall stand by you with a devotion that no foreigner can approach, ready to lay down our lives, if need be, in defense of yours, interlacing our industrial, commercial, civil, and religious life with yours in a way that shall make the interests of both races one.

Booker T Washington
1895

The answers to the challenges of the black community in the United States are complicated at times. It is a fact that the crime rates in predominantly black communities are disproportionately high. But, though I will never condone crimes of any type for any reason, there are certainly things that aid in the decisions to drive a person to illegal activities.

One of the things to keep in mind is that economically distraught communities often carry with them high crime rates. So, with all of the complicated issues in underprivileged communities, one issue is very simple. Jobs, or the lack of jobs, is a driving force for crime rates.

One of the biggest challenges to the employment of blacks is the country's approach to immigration. It is simply amazing that many of those claiming to be advocates for the black community are also in favor of opening our borders to illegal immigrants.

We are a nation of immigrants; however, the fact is that

there are only so many jobs to go around. You don't have to be a mathematician to understand that if there is a small community of 15,000 people and everyone there has a job, then you add 5,000 workers to the population, someone is going to lose their job or not get one.

Once again, decisions are made that have a tremendous effect on the black community with no real thought of how they are affected.

A brilliant scholar who did tremendous work in this area is Jacquelyne Johnson Jackson. Much of what you are about to read is directly from her. She passed away in 2004, but her writings on the subject are more relevant than ever.

Among other things, she stressed:

1) the impact of legal and illegal immigrants on blacks in low-wage jobs in the secondary labor market
2) the attitudes of blacks toward immigration reform before passage of the immigration law
3) the likely impact of the act on blacks living in areas with high concentrations of recent immigrants and refugees.

Labor market statistics and simple observations have historically shown a pronounced trend of immigrant and refugee workers replacing many native black unskilled, semi-skilled and supervisory workers in such businesses as hotels, restaurants, fast food outlets, light manufacturing firms, construction firms, and taxicab companies in metropolitan areas with heavy concentrations of immigrants. Many studies have suggested that undocumented workers displace low-skilled workers and depress wages within the black community.

Illegal immigrants are concentrated in the major urban areas which are also occupied by black citizens and in industries and occupations where blacks have been overrepresented.

Five of the top ten urban black population centers

(Chicago, Houston, Los Angeles, New York and Washington, D.C.) are also the areas where the most illegal immigrants have settled. Even those who believe that immigrants don't displace a significant number of native workers on a nationwide scale agree that, in areas heavily populated by immigrants, steep competition between similarly skilled immigrants and native workers can be significant.

It has been demonstrated that illegal workers tend to dominate certain work forces because immigrants eventually gain control of mid-level supervisory positions and job recruitment. From this vantage point illegal immigrants, through their networks of family and friends often "beat others to the punch," so to speak, and land jobs otherwise given to the black community.

Job networks that are control-led by immigrants, and in turn hire other immigrants, have particularly harmed the employment prospects of blacks who look for jobs by using their friends and relatives.

Almost one-fifth of unemployed blacks typically use fewer than two job-seeking methods. They most often rely upon their friends and relatives. Employment sectors, once filled by black workers, have become dominated by immigrants receiving low wages.

One factor that is often overlooked is that blacks have been increasingly shut out of jobs because of "linguistic" discrimination. In Florida for instance, many hotels and other service employers now hire only Spanish-speaking or bilingual workers. These employers often perceive a lack of "fit" between blacks and their Spanish-speaking employees and customers.

A growing number of local school districts and public agencies in areas with heavy concentrations of immigrants are hiring fewer people who speak only one language. Many black professionals who are fluent only in English are now losing out to bilingual competitors.

There is certainly a debate as to how much illegal

immigration affects the black community. There is controversy about the effects of immigrants and refugees on native black employment and earnings, though I believe data and common sense tells us there is certainly an effect.

But blacks deserve the benefit of the doubt. Public policies should be shaped by values that promote economic equity for all citizens, including those Americans whose slave ancestors did not come to American shores in search of freedom.

I am simply amazed that a representative of a predominantly black population can, with a straight face, speak of racism when negatively addressing the need to prevent further illegal immigration.

Where is the common sense when a city predominantly black, with a high unemployment rate, chooses to push for the acceptance of many thousands of illegal immigrants?

It is easy to be generous with the jobs and the livelihood of others. To those generous politicians, however, I would say, "Take care of the people you currently represent." Protect them. Fight for a better life for them.

When their jobs are taken away crime rates go up. Families cannot afford to feed themselves, and despair is common. At the risk of being redundant, it is not rocket science to understand that, in their communities, there is already a lack of jobs. To allow people to break the law and come into those communities looking for work cannot and will not help the wonderful people living there who are already struggling to survive.

How easy is it to understand that if there are three jobs available with three people fighting for it, their chances are minimized if five more people looking for work come into that community.

Finally, the influx of people into this country illegally has not really been a point of disagreement over the years. Whether people from other countries should be able to come to America legally has never been a point of disagreement at all. Virtually everyone is for that. Whether people from other countries should be allowed to come into the country illegally has not historically ever been challenged until recently. Some people have been very harsh in their opinions, but most have just had strong opinions.

Here are a few of those opinions:

"We simply cannot allow people to pour into the United States undetected, undocumented, unchecked, and circumventing the line of people who are waiting patiently, diligently, and lawfully to become immigrants in this country."

---Barack Obama, 2005

All Americans, not only in the states most heavily affected but in every place in this country, are rightly disturbed by the large numbers of illegal aliens entering our country.

The jobs they hold might otherwise be held by citizens or legal immigrants. The public services they use impose burdens on our taxpayers. That's why our administration has moved aggressively to secure our borders more by hiring a record number of new border guards, by deporting twice as many criminal aliens as ever before, by cracking down on illegal hiring, by barring welfare benefits to illegal aliens.

We are a nation of immigrants. But we are also a nation of laws. It is wrong and ultimately self-defeating for a nation of immigrants to permit the kind of abuse of our immigration laws we have seen in recent years, and we must do more to stop it.

--- Bill Clinton, 1995

"Those who enter the country illegally and those who employ them disrespect the rule of law, and they are showing disregard for those who are following the law. We simply cannot allow people to pour into the United States undetected, undocumented (and) unchecked, and circumventing the line of people who are waiting patiently, diligently and lawfully to become immigrants in this country."

---Barack Obama

"Our administration has moved aggressively to secure our borders more by hiring a record number of new border guards, by deporting twice as many criminal aliens as ever before, by cracking down on illegal hiring, by barring welfare benefits to illegal aliens."

---Bill Clinton

"If making it easy to be an illegal alien isn't enough, how about offering an award to be an illegal immigrant. No sane country would do that, right? Guess again."

--- Sen. Harry Reid, D-Nev.

"In approaching immigration reform, I believe we must enact tough, practical reforms that ensure and promote the legal and orderly entry of immigrants into our country."

---Barack Obama

"We all agree on the need to better secure the border, and to punish employers who choose to hire illegal immigrants."

--- Barack Obama

"We will try to do more to speed the deportation of illegal aliens who are arrested for crimes, to better identify illegal aliens in the workplace."

--- Bill Clinton

"I continue to believe that we need stronger enforcement on the border and at the workplace. And that means a workable mandatory system that employers must use to verify the legality of their workers."

--- Barack Obama

"If you break our laws by entering this country without permission and give birth to a child, we reward that child with U.S. citizenship and guarantee full access to all public and social services this society provides — and that's a lot of services. Is it any wonder that two-thirds of babies born at taxpayer expense (in) county-run hospitals in Los Angeles are born to illegal alien mothers?"

--- Harry Reid

"We need to start by giving agencies charged with border security new technology, new facilities and more people to stop, process and deport illegal immigrants."

--- Barack Obama

"Right now we've got millions of illegal immigrants who live and work here without knowing their identity or background."

--- Barack Obama

"Let me repeat: We need strong border security at the borders."

--- Barack Obama

"There are too many (migrants) now. ... Europe, for example, Germany, cannot become an Arab country. Germany is Germany. ... From a moral point of view, too, I think refugees should only be admitted temporarily."

--- Dalai Llama

We cannot let illegals think that their children will get to stay here just because they make it across the border.

--- Hillary Clinton

CHAPTER IV
War On Black Families

"What else can we do? We are losing our streets. These young people are not just normal young people. They are literally "super-predators.""

"I'm sorry," Mark says to Bob. "I'm not familiar with that term. What exactly is a "super-predator?""

"You know, they have no conscience, no empathy."

"How can we deal with them? How did they come about?"

*"Well," Bob says, "we can talk about why they ended up that way, but first, we have to **bring them to heel**."*

"Bring them to heel?" says Mark. "I'm feeling really stupid, but that's another term I just don't understand."

"To be blunt, it means to 'force them to obey.' The term refers to commanding a dog to come close behind its master. You know, how a human makes a dog heel. We need to make them heel"

"How exactly are we going to do that? It's a pretty big task."

"We do it the same way we fought the mob. We have to launch an organized effort against gangs. We need to take these people on. They're often connected to big drug cartels. They're not just gangs of kids anymore."

"Have we made any progress getting these people under control?"

"Yeah, we're making some progress, There has been some success with 'community policing.' The Crime Bill Act passed back in 1994 finally got more police officers on the streets. That is something at least."

The reference is to the 1994 Violent Crime Control and Law Enforcement Act was signed into law by Bill Clinton. Among other things, it put a ban on some assault weapons. It provided more funding for community policing and an expansion of the death penalty. The legislation was championed by Bill Clinton as a way to reduce the number of African Americans being killed in drug-related incidents.

The Act, however, put a disproportionately large number of young black men into prison. Of all the things the act called for, three stick out.

1. Authorized the death penalty for 60 new federal offenses

Whether you believe in the death penalty or not the statistics are firm in showing that the death penalty has always terrorized black communities. The crime bill's Federal Death Penalty Act permitted the use of the death penalty for 60 new federal offenses, including certain drug offences not related to a homicide. In the five years following the bill's passage, 44 percent of defendants with death penalty recommendations from federal prosecutors were black. Another 21 percent were Hispanic.

I have tried to make a point that, while the term racism has been used in instances that are often blown out of proportion, far worst atrocities have been ignored completely. Certain acts have been legitimately used to thin out the population with little to no push-back. Basically, the idea has been to "make them heel or kill them."

2. Imposed mandatory life sentences for individuals with three or more felony convictions

The crime bill implemented a rash of new three-strikes laws: laws that impose automatic life sentences for people convicted of certain felony offenses if they already have two convictions on their record.

The crime bill's three-strikes provision sent thousands of Americans to prison for life based on previous offenses for minor crimes such as stealing loose change from a parked car. In 2016, <u>78.5 percent</u> of Americans serving life sentences in federal prison were black.

In Maryland, Mississippi, and Louisiana; black people alone constitute approximately three-quarters of those sentenced to life in prison. The federal government recently replaced its mandatory life sentence with a 25-year minimum sentence; however, hundreds of Americans will die in prison as a result of the three-strikes law.

So, once again, while the focus continues to be on events that, at times, cannot be backed up with true statistics; we see young black men "thinned out" by putting them in jail for life, or just executing them.

3. Levied harsh new penalties for justice-involved youth

In an attempt to make the super-predators heel, it was made easier to prosecute individuals at a younger age. This took a large number of young black men from school to prison: low-income children of color, especially black students, who were convicted of multiple crimes.

Among other things, the crime bill allowed prosecutors to charge 13-year-old children as adults for certain crimes. As a result, today, <u>two-thirds</u> of Americans who were sentenced to life in prison as juveniles are black.

The bill also called for sentencing enhancements for youth who are convicted of certain offenses and believed to be associated with gangs. Law enforcement report that more than 90 percent of gang members are black.

Conclusion

The legacy of the Violent Crime Control and Law Enforcement Act of 1994 continues to harm black People in so many ways. Many of those responsible for it are now leading us to believe they are the ones who can fix things.

CHAPTER V
Strategy

Conversation One:
"Man, it is so good to see you. I've been a fan forever."

"Hey, same here. What you guys are doing today is just crazy. It's a different game. Anyway, what are your chances? It's looking pretty good for you isn't it?"

"Well, a lot could go wrong, but I think we have a great chance to win it all. That's what I wanted to talk about. If we play like we can, there's no reason anyone can beat us. I've been thinking about it. Millions of people will watch us. Kids will buy our shoes. We'll be on talk shows and maybe even write books. You know. You've been there."

"Oh man, your life will get crazy. But how can I help?"

"Some of us have talked. This may be the only '15 minutes of fame' we will ever get. I hope not, but how do we use this? We want to change communities. We want more for the black community."

"Great. Well, you've come to the right place. There is something I've been working on for a long time. This is so big they'll make a holiday of this event."

"Hey, I'm in. What do you have?"

"When you win, the President of the United States will invite you to the White House. Are you ready for this? Don't go."

"Really? That's not too radical is it?"

"Think of what will happen if you do this. Racism will stop dead in its tracks. Our people will stop killing each other. The government will immediately put money into schools, and into educating the police. This will be truly epic."

Conversation Two:

"Man, it is so good to see you. I've been a fan forever."

"Hey, same here. What you guys are doing today is just crazy. It's a different game. Anyway, what are your chances? It's looking pretty good for you."

"Well, a lot could go wrong, but I think we have a great chance to win it all. That's what I wanted to talk about. If we play like we can, there's no reason anyone can beat us. I've been thinking about it. Millions of people will watch us. Kids will buy our shoes. We'll be on talk shows and maybe even write books. You know. You've been there."

"Oh man, your life will get crazy. But how can I help?"

"Some of us have talked. This may the only '15 minutes of fame' we will ever get. I hope not, but how do we use this? We want to change communities. We want more for the black community."

"Great. Well, you've come to the right place. There is something I've been working on for a long time. This is so big they'll make a holiday of this event."

"Hey, I'm in. What do you have?"

"Think about what the NBA could do. Each year the NBA makes approximately 30 new black millionaires. Every year. The average salary for an NBA player is about $8,000,000.00. Ten players are making over $30M per year. With 30 teams and 15 players on a team each year NBA players make a combined total of $3,600,000,000.00."

"Yeah, we are doing quite well if I do say so myself."

"Do you realize that, if we somehow managed to get each player to give 10% of their salaries, $360M could be given each year? I realize it is a big sacrifice. You would somehow have to learn to live off of $36M a year. All kidding aside, $360M could really help our communities.

"Wow, that could do some real good."

"But listen. You are going to be invited to the White House. Ask for an hour extra of the president's time to discuss things. What if you suggested we are creating this foundation? It's geared to help our communities get on their feet. Ask him if the government could help. Ask him to give a match each year of the player's contribution. Then ask the owners to match our numbers each year as well. If we could pull this off, we are looking at $1B each year. If we then ask for donations during every televised game, who knows what we may take in? With that much money, we can provide education, job-training, and even job placement. We can change a lot of things."

"Who would run it?'

"Listen, we have some great business minds in our ranks. We have men who have been working in inner cities for years. We literally have household names within us. We can also draw from other professional athletes. Can you imagine? Magic Johnson, Jim Brown, Kareem, Jerry Rice, etc. This could be huge."

"Wow, I thought you were going to tell me to not go to the White House, or to put a message on my uniform."

CHAPTER VI
Killing Thousands

"We need this to happen," Bob says. "If we don't, the population of the low-income, feebleminded, the criminals will grow out of control. We can't take it. Our economy can't take it. We have to monitor and control these populations."

"But how?" Mark asks. "We've pushed birth-control. We've sterilized them. Yet, they keep having kids."

"Yes, and these kids are costing us a fortune. We're paying for their housing; we're paying for their food. We're sending them checks each month that get larger every time they have another child. Our prisons are full. To make matters worse, they're pushing back. As the public becomes more aware as to what we've been doing, there will be more and more of an uproar. The stories are getting out. It doesn't matter anyway; these programs have not seen the results we so desperately need."

"Then what?"

"We need abortion to be legalized. We need it to be accepted, accessible, and promoted. We need a clinic on the corner of every low-income community in the country. Some larger inner cities need 4-5 clinics. We need to make going in for an abortion as easy and as acceptable as going in for a flu shot. Over the next 35 years, we need to see 19,000,000 black babies aborted. That will mean, by 2020, there will be roughly 35 million less blacks than if we don't do that.

This, along with an aggressive birth control program, just might keep these numbers at a workable number."

"But how in the world will we ever get them to agree to this?" Mark asks. "These are their babies we are talking about."

"You're kidding right?" says Bob. "They will fight with all their strength to make this happen. They'll do what we tell them to do."

Fast forward:

"Look, we're in a real bind here. We simply cannot afford to take care of these black families. More and more of their families don't have a man in the house. That means we're the new dad. It is now up to us to provide housing, food, and a modest income. Where is this money going to come from?"

"What are you suggesting?" Mark says.

"I'm suggesting," says Bob, "that we need to take advantage of the legalization of abortion and help to convince these people an abortion is a good option. They are not going to continue to tolerate the sterilizations we've been performing. We've jammed birth control completely down their throats. Every single time we provide for them in any way they get educated again on birth control."

"Do you really think they will be open to abortions? These people have a strong history of family. I just don't see it."

"Well, it will be a process. We will first need to run it through an organization separate from the government. We don't need all these watchdog groups looking over our shoulders every minute. Then we need this organization to set up facilities in and around our low-income communities. We need this organization to be THE place for young black women to go for counsel and help, to be the place that can relieve them of their 'problem' in just one visit."

"I don't know. It seems like we're banking on this quite a bit. What if it doesn't work?"

"Well, let's put it this way, if something isn't done, by the year 2020, the population of blacks in this country will exceed 70 million. Forget feeding, clothing, and housing them; they will decide a lot of elections."

"But how are you going to get them to accept this? A lot of people, especially in the black community, feel as though abortion is murder.

I'm not sure they will accept this."

"Accept it? When we're done, they will be holding signs demanding the right for an abortion. They will vote for any and every candidate who pushes for it. In so doing, we will rid this country of tens of millions of them."

Abortion impacts African Americans at a higher rate than any other population group. In 2011, the Centers for Disease Control and Prevention released an Abortion Surveillance Report. According to that report, black women make up 14 percent of the childbearing population. Yet, 36 percent of all abortions were obtained by black women. At a ratio of 474 abortions per 1,000 live births, black women have the highest ratio of any group in the country.

Those percentages indicate that, of the over 44 million abortions since the 1973 *Roe vs Wade* Supreme Court ruling, 19 million black babies have been aborted. African Americans are just over 13 percent of the United States population. The population of blacks in 1973 was roughly 23,000,000. Today it is 40,000,000. It is difficult to estimate what the population would be had there have been no abortions in the black community.

If we estimate the number of offspring that would have been born from those 19,000,000 it is safe to say the current population of blacks would be at least 65,000,000. By manipulating the black community into choosing abortions, the US has saved hundreds of millions of dollars.

Corrections currently cost $81B per year. From 1970-2013 the corrections budget in this country quadruped from $17B to $71B. Blacks make up 40% of all of those incarcerated. Therefore, reducing the black population saves millions and millions of dollars each year.

The total amount of spending each year for the 83 federal welfare programs in this country is $1,030,000,000,000.00. (One trillion dollars) Currently 41.6% of the black population participate in welfare programs. Since approximately 40% of those on some type of welfare program in this country are black, reducing the black population saves the US billions and billions of dollars each year.

White women are five times less likely to have an abortion than black women. Why? Perhaps it is a matter of availability. A study by Protecting Black Lives, in 2012, found that 79 percent of Planned Parenthood's surgical abortion facilities are located within walking distance of minority communities.

The prevalence of abortion providers in African American and Hispanic neighborhoods indicates the abortion industry is targeting both groups. It smacks of the eugenics-linked past of Planned Parenthood founder Margaret Sanger and her views of contraception and abortion as ways of diminishing the black population.

The impacts on our black communities are hard to fathom. According to the Guttmacher Institute, which generally supports abortion, 360,000 black babies were aborted in 2011. CDC statistics for 2011 show that 287,072 black deaths occurred from all other causes excluding abortion. By these numbers, abortion is the leading cause of death among blacks.

Dr. Kermit Gosnell was an abortionist in the Philadelphia area who was charged with the murder of a woman who had died from a botched abortion. He was also charged for several "live birth" abortions in which the baby was born alive and then killed.

You would think such a horrific occurrence would be a big news story. When he went to trial, the press gallery was empty. Kermit Gosnell's abortion mill was in a black community.

The news media did not care.

CHAPTER VII
Killing Me Softly

Note: For the following two chapters I simply cannot give enough credit to Mark Crutcher, president of Life Dynamics and his work with Maafa 21.

NIXON Tape #697-29:
Nixon: "*A majority of people in Colorado voted for abortion, I think a majority of people in Michigan are for abortion, I think in both cases, well, certainly in Michigan they will vote for it because they think that what's going to be aborted generally are the* **little black bastards**."

NIXON TAPE 700-10:
Nixon: " *… as I told you and we talked about it earlier, that a hell of a lot of people want to* **control all the Negro bastards**."
Unidentified Staff: "*Yeah*"

White House Tape 700/10 – April 3, 1972:
Nixon: ... you know what we are talking about – population control.
Unidentified staffer: Sure

Maafa 21
Www.Maafa 21.com

In the early 1800's, slaves were an asset to the wealthy elite in the South. Once free, they became a liability. Every aspect of the economy was invested in the slave business. Four million uneducated people who were unemployable anywhere except in cotton fields were soon to be unleashed. The potential to bankrupt the economy was more than just a remote possibility.

The north was concerned about migration. Potentially, four million people who had no marketable skills could come North. They had virtually no possessions. They had nowhere to live. There was concern over racial purity. There were many who simply wanted to send former slaves back from where they came. They were now free; just take them back and drop them off. This was called Colonization.

What to do? It was called the negro dilemma. To many, the best solution was simply to limit their numbers. The more black people reproduced, the worse things would be. So, it seemed to make sense. Control the population.

Francis Galton, a cousin of Charles Darwin, summed up what most people believed at the time when he wrote, "average negroes possess too little intellect, self-reliance, and self-control to make it possible for them to sustain the burden of any respectable form of civilization without a large measure of external guidance and support."

A movement started. It was alive and well in the US. It was a movement to determine the birth of only the very best. It was a movement that would encourage the brightest and best, those of high moral character, etc. to reproduce and increase in population. The undesirable populations were to have their numbers limited.

So, a strategy was put into place. Encourage white people to have more and more children. This was called "positive eugenics". Limit the population of blacks by encouraging and teaching birth control, making birth-control available and affordable, and forcing sterilization.

Because blacks were seen as feebleminded, criminal, unfit, imbeciles and immoral; blacks were asked to commit racial suicide.

The white elites backed the program with strategy and with money. They had made a lot of money with slaves and, now that slaves had been given their freedom, they were ready to spend that money to bring about their extinction.

They remained in the shadows, however. They didn't want to be seen. So, organizations were formed and a "front man," a crusader if you will, was chosen. Her name was Margaret Sanger. She would found *The American Birth Control League* and publish its newsletter, *The Birth Control Review*.

The eugenics movement, that movement to see the best races, and people aggressively reproduce while less desirables limited their reproduction, was launched in the United States. It was held together by race and class.

Eugenics was believed by many to be the best thing to deal with the "negro problem."

The organization at the heart of it was *The American Birth Control League*. Throughout this section I will refer to them not only during the time that they went by that name but also beyond. That way, we cannot have our opinions be developed by prejudice for them or against them.

It was clear that, from the beginning, to those involved in the eugenics movement - black lives did not matter.

Before attempting to put forth my opinion, however, I will simply provide quotes of those who were involved with *The American Birth Control League* and in what was called the "eugenics movement".

"The problem of the socially fit must be treated not as one of color but as a problem of the spread of feeble mindedness."

Dr. Davenport
1913 Director of The Eugenics Record Office
Co-founder American Eugenics Society

"We are paying for and even submitting to the dictates of an ever-increasing class of humans that never should have been born at all."

Margaret Sanger
founder of *The American Birth Control League*
"The laws of nature requires the obliteration of the unfit and human life is valuable only when it is of use to the community or race"

Madison Grant
co-founder of *The American Eugenics Society*

"The practice of birth control among the majority of colored people would probably be more eugenic than among their white counterparts. The dissemination of the information of birth control should have begun with this class other than the upper social and economic class."
Birth Control Review

"In virtually every community where negroes dwell one finds them in fat times and lean alike contributing a disproportionate number to the rolls of the defendants and delinquents They make excessive demands on the white man's charity and over tax his patience."
Newell's Sims Birth Control Review - 1932

"The leader of the German nation, Adolf Hitler, has been able to construct a comprehensive racial policy of population development and improvement." "The difference between the Jew and the Arian is as insurmountable as that between black and white...Germany has set a pattern which other nations must follow."
Dr. Clarence Gordon Campbell
president of *The American Eugenics Research association NY*

"Non-Whites are excluded from America"
Lothrop Stoddard
Director, *The American Birth Control League*

- Lothrop Stoddard, the Director of *The American Birth Control League* met with both Adolf Hitler and Heinrich
- *The American Birth Control League* headed the movement to limit the reproduction of inferior groups (eugenics)
- Code words were used. *The American Birth Control League* was seeking to eliminate criminals, feeble-minded, poor, and the impoverished.
- Adolph Hitler was influenced by those in the US promoting the eugenics movement.
- Nazi school textbooks featured the philosophy of Lothrop Stoddard director of *The American Birth Control League.*
- On 1927 Eugene Fisher called for the eradication of blacks at the World Population Conference
- Harry Laughlin, an official for the American Eugenics Society and *The American Birth Control League* mailed out letters to 3,000 biology teachers urging them to show the Nazis Eugenic Film in English to their students.
- In 1936 Harry Laughlin published plans for forced sterilization against degenerate offspring in the Birth Control Review
- Laughlin was praised in a Nazis newspaper for his contribution to the Nazi Eugenics effort. He was awarded an honorary degree in Heidelberg.
- In the 1930's a German psychiatrist named Ernst Ruden was named president of the International Federation of Eugenics. In 1933 Ruden's call for racial purity was published in the Birth Control Review.
- Adolf Hitler chose Reden to write Germany's eugenics laws.
- Concentration camps were to be at least partially patterned after the American Eugenics movement.

- At Indiana in 1919, 300,000 workers were put in a colony of the feebleminded.
- Margaret Sanger stressed for a need for farms and open spaces where "the illiterate, unemployed and poor should be sent there."
- In 1935 Germany sterilized 600 women who had fathered children by black men and recommended the sterilization of all negro and hybrid races.
- American Eugenics Society Walter Ashley Plecker wrote a letter to the German betterment of eugenics and praised them expressing his hope not one child had been missed. Ten years earlier he wrote that blacks were the greatest problem and most destructive force which confronts the white race and American civilization.

Frederick Osborne explained that the goals of controlling the population of the feebleminded, criminals, etc., were going to need to be championed under the name of something other than eugenics. The president and founding member of the American Eugenics Society and *The American Birth Control League* was concerned over the connection to Nazis and to phrases like population control. They initiated the use of terms such as "Planning".

Those involved were obsessed with race. In the 1920's Margaret Sanger tried to merge *The American Birth Control League* with the *American Eugenics Society*. She managed to combine their publications stressing that eugenics and birth control had the same goals.

Margaret Sanger spoke at a KKK gathering in NJ. Afterwards she bragged that after that speech she was invited by 12 other chapters to speak.

"Commonly it is considered a great misfortune for America that Negro slaves were ever imported. The presence of Negro's in America today is usually considered a plight on the nation."

"All white Americans agree that if the Negro is to be eliminated

he must be eliminated slowly so as not to hurt any living individual Negros."

"The only possible way of decreasing Negro populations is by means of controlling fertility."

"Birth control facilities could be extended relatively more to Negroes than to whites. Since Negroes are more concentrated in lower income and education classes.

Gunner Myrdal

Gunner Myrdal was a man involved in Eugenics. Gunner thought blacks could not help themselves and that no one could. Therefore, we should get rid of them.

Between 1790 and 1940 the Negro population increased 17 times. The white population increased 37 times. Yet, there was no talk of the need to slow the growth of the white population.

"We will do it by force"

Donald Winkler, 1972
President of the American Assoc. of Planned Parenthood
Physicians and BOD member.

"The world and almost our civilization for the next 25 years is going to depend upon a cheap, safe contraceptive to be used in poverty stricken areas, slums, jungles, most ignorant people. Even this will not be sufficient. We need a national sterilization for certain types of our population who are being encouraged to breed and would die out if the government didn't feed them."

Margaret Sanger
founder of *The American Birth Control League*
"Three generations of imbeciles is enough."

Oliver Wendell Holmes

In 1934 Adolf Hitler complimented León Whitney on a book he wrote. Whitney was a writer for The Birth Control Review.

The Eugenics movement believed that feeble-mindedness was hereditary. Therefore, children as young as eight-year-old were sterilized.

Oliver Wendell Holmes once wrote, *"Three generations of imbeciles is enough."*

In 1907 thirty states had sterilization laws.

In Oregon in the 1970's, 60,000 people were sterilized, mostly black.

In 1972 one third of Medicaid patients were sterilized.

The state of NJ said sterilization was needed for the economy.

In 1939, the American Birth Control League founded by Margaret Sanger, merged with the first legal birth control clinic in the US, the Birth Control Clinical Research Bureau. (The Birth Control Clinical Research Bureau had previously been called the Clinical Research Bureau and changed its name after Margaret Sanger gained control of it.)

In 1942 the Birth Control Federation of America changed its name to what we all know it as now: Planned Parenthood Federation of America.

Planned Parenthood was not so much born but came forth as the final creation of all of those working in the movement to see to it that only the brightest and best would increase in population.

By 1969, when the number of sterilizations approved by the Iowa State Eugenics Board began to decrease, Planned Parenthood attacked them. Robert Weber said, "Increase or quit."

CHAPTER VIII
To Go Where Lots of Men
Have Gone Before

It is by far the most exciting thing you have ever done.

Is this really happening? Is time travel real? Is space travel real?

You have volunteered and been chosen to try out a top secret "ship".

They are somewhat vague as to where you are going. They are hoping to jet you across the universe. They have said you may actually travel through time.

They will put you to sleep and, once you wake up, you will be in a strange place. It is possible that you may even end up in a place very similar to where you are now. You may experience another world like ours. You may come face to face with your doppelgänger.

You say goodbye to your friends and family.

Today is the day.

You are put to sleep. You may be asleep for 25 days or 25 years.

Regardless, it will seem as though you have just fallen asleep. You will wake up in a different world.

The chances of you coming back are real but slim.

Once in the ship you are slowly put to sleep.

And then…you wake up.

As you depart your ship, you are relieved that where you have gone is not a lot different than where you left. You are relieved that you can breathe the air. As you wander into the city you hear people speaking your language. They are dressed for the most part like you. You even find a coffee shop. As you listen to the two people talking beside you, you are excited to hear that they are talking about the advancement society has made.

"This is the most advanced society at the most advanced time in history," they say.

What a relief. You are filled with excitement.

What to do now?

As you continue to wander, you are approached by a young man. He asked if you are lost. You quickly make up a story. Your car broke down and you have walked into town. You are looking to get a bite to eat and get some help with your car. This young man offers his help, along with that of his mother. He offers to take you to her place of work where you can wait until she gets off.

You enter this nice building and meet his mother. She is a very nice lady and offers to let you "take the tour" while you wait.

You are placed in a room. At some point you wander out to go to the restroom. You overhear a conversation coming from a room. Since you are there to gather information, you stop to listen. It goes like this:

"I am excited to contribute to your organization. You are doing such good work."

"Well thank you. We are very proud of our work. It is very rewarding."

"I'm sure it is. I do want to make sure I understand how this works. As we discussed, I am very interested in seeing my contribution go toward the black community. So again, that is not a problem?"

"Oh no, not at all. We have a lot of people that direct

their contributions. If that is where you want it to go, that is where it will go."

"That is very refreshing to hear. So, if I want to direct this all to four or five or ten black families you will see that it gets there?"

"Absolutely. You have my word."

How refreshing. This is a very advanced society. You are glad they seem to not have racial challenges like the ones back home.

After your restroom break, you make it back to a room where a nice young man is starting a video presentation. He explains that there are several segments, and each person is allowed to watch all or none of them.

The video starts.

A woman is introduced as the founder of the organization. It was started decades ago. The film is in black and white. This woman seems intelligent. She talks of her work in population control. She explains the need to control populations around the world and the significance of limiting certain races and making sure the superior races continue to grow.

She discusses her work with Germans and their program of not only limiting certain races but in getting rid of them all together. She even explains what needs to be done if we are to completely do away with the black population.

This seemingly well-educated woman explains how the black population especially produces imbeciles, and criminals and people that, left to themselves without white people supporting them, cannot survive.

This organization, *The Birth Control League,* is leading the move to limit the number of black people not only in this country but in others. They are doing this by educating the unintelligent in birth control and in many cases having young black women sterilized.

She expresses how this has to be forced in many cases. She stresses how, in the future, more aggressive steps will need to be taken to limit certain populations, including the black community. She is very proud of this movement and the organization she has founded. Her work has been studied and supported by the Nazis in Germany and by the KKK in this country.

You are shocked to say the least. You fully expect someone to interrupt and explain how the current organization has confronted her and led the charge against her. Instead, those around the room are nodding in approval. After her presentation, there is a rousing round of applause. There is a break, and anyone interested is invited back for the next segment.

What has happened? Where are you?

During the break you quickly open the literature you have been given. You find that millions upon millions of unborn babies have been murdered.

But there is more to it than that.

By doing some quick calculations, you find that, though the black community makes up roughly 13% of the population, 19 million, almost 40% of the abortions done in this country, were done to black babies.

A map showing the location of the various abortion clinics reveals that they are overwhelmingly within walking distance of black communities as though blacks are somehow being targeted.

The words of this woman are almost prophetic. By limiting the number of babies born in the black communities, this organization has been successful in controlling the black population while allowing the white population to expand with no limitations.

Her dreams are being realized.

You are weak in your knees. How can this be?

It is now time to start the next segment.

You are shown videos of babies being aborted. At times limbs are torn off of the baby. The mother has a procedure to limit the pain, but the baby has none. At times a poison is injected into the baby much like a lethal injection for someone on death row.

The baby struggles, opens wide its mouth as if to scream, and dies.

Sometimes the babies are cut into small pieces and removed one piece at a time.

You observe surgeries that are performed to harvest body parts of the babies.

You find out that this organization obtains a great deal of its funding by selling these body parts.

You find out that, during a period of time, what is known as "partial birth abortions" were legal. In one example of this, a full-term baby's body was partially delivered. Before its head was brought out of the mother, a cut was made on the back of the baby's neck. A tube then sucked out the baby's brain.

It was legal under the premise that, until the baby was fully born, with even one body part not delivered, it was not yet a life.

This procedure was banned by Congress in 2003. The Supreme Court upheld the ban in 2007.

Within the video, however, there is an explanation as to how they have found ways around the law.

They are proud of this because it is the only way to harvest certain body parts for sale and distribution.

There are videos shown of the "great work" they are doing by showing the eyeballs, livers, kidneys, and hearts of these unborn babies taken and put in a tray.

They are then carried out and delivered to the buyer.

Of great interest to you is the disproportionate number of black babies that are seen in the video. This is not so much the sheer number of abortions but the number of black babies in comparison to the overall population.

Black babies are killed, often mutilated, and have had body parts surgically removed for what must be an overwhelmingly number of white people.

You run from the room.

You sprint to the first door that is labeled exit.

You barely make it outside as you begin to vomit.

The picture of a baby being born dead with his eyes having been removed is something you will never be able to get out of your mind.

As you continue to throw up, you notice the large silver container that you have put your hand on to steady yourself. As you pull yourself up and look in it you see in it dozens of dead babies. Half are white, and slightly less than half are black.

There are babies missing arms and legs. There are babies sliced down the middle showing no internal organs.

There is one baby that sticks out at you. It still has its thumb in its mouth.

There are two black twins laying beside each other as if taken in their sleep and laid there.

You are quickly escorted inside, being told you are not to be out there. This is where the "fetuses" are taken before being removed from the property.

You are reminded that each fetus you have seen represents a tremendous service this organization does for hurting individuals. Without them, these women would have nowhere to go.

You are reminded that this organization is responsible for 330,000 of these abortions a year. What surprises you the most is that you are told this with great pride and enthusiasm.

In somewhat of a stupor you walk to the front of the building.

Where have you come to? What type of society are you in? How could you have ended up in such a place?

As you walk outside, you wander down a street and recognize the facility you have so often come to. It is then you realize that the "ship" didn't work. You went nowhere. You are home.

Welcome to the United States of America 2020. Welcome to Planned Parenthood.

CHAPTER IX
Open Their Eyes so They May See

I enjoy magic. I am often amazed as I watch it. The way I understand it, it's all about "misdirection". If somehow our attention can be directed elsewhere the "magic" can happen. I'm sure many people reading this have tried everything they can not to be drawn in another direction while watching an act of magic.

With that in mind, I want to ask you to concentrate. We have come so far to this point. I realize that, in dealing with the topic of abortion, I have run the risk of facing the wrath of those who desperately try to take our focus off of black genocide in this country.

So please, as voices come out of the woodwork to attack me and this book on the topic of abortion, focus. **Abortion and the legalization of abortion has virtually everything to do with population control of the black community in this country.**

Debate the topic of legalized abortion another time. I will be glad to; however, if you get nothing else from this book, remember that nothing has done more harm to the black community in this country than abortion has.

In terms of the population of whites and blacks in this country, there is a horribly disproportionate number of abortions within the black community. If there had never been an abortion of a black baby in the US, the black population would now be somewhere around 65,000,000 people. Abortion has stripped black people of one of their greatest weapons – their numbers.

A larger black population means more power in elections. A larger black population means greater buying power. A greater black population means a larger influence in politics, education, sports, and business. As it stands, the black population in the US represents the eighteenth largest economy in the world. Abortion in the US has drained the influence of 65,000,000 people to the influence of 40,000,000.

Think about that for a moment.

There are 197,181,177 white people in America. What differences would there be if there were 65,000,000 blacks compared to 40,000,000 blacks in this country?

So little thought or effort has been put into this because we have been the victims of misdirection.

Every life is important. Fighting for each life is important. Yet when a person with a criminal record, who has raped, committed assault, and who has been in and out of prison loses his or her life, there are thousands of media hours given to it.

I'm not saying there shouldn't be. On the other hand, when a seventeen-year-old young black girl is targeted with millions of dollars from the American people to kill her unborn baby, nothing appears in this same media.

As a matter of fact, millions of dollars are used to convince the black community that those controlling their population have their best interest at heart.

Focus has been taken off of a vast program to limit the number of black people not only in this country but in the world.

One of the greatest driving forces behind this, without knowing they are doing so, is the black community in America.

To add insult to injury, the people who have, for decades, worked to limit the black population, are passionately supported by the black community. There have been thousands and thousands of black people that have been used to support people who support a system that kills more blacks in four days than the KKK has in 150 years.

They can't do it without the black community.

While the masses of black people stand on a corner fighting desperately for justice, a thousand young black women somehow walk pregnant into a building and leave crying, only to go home alone and deal with what has happened.

Yet few fight for them. Few support them. Money is not directed to them in their biggest time of need.

Misdirection.

CHAPTER X
Just My Opinion

There are levels of commitment for everything. It's easy to say we are passionate about something, but words are cheap. Levels of commitment range from

1) Talk

2) Campaign or protest

3) Support with your time

4) Donations. (With giving money one of the greatest shows of commitment.)

Again, talk is cheap.

That is obviously simplistic and can be debated.

But what is real commitment to a cause?

Schindler's List is the true story of a man who gave every dime he had to keep others alive. At the risk of being offensive, it is one thing to take a knee for a cause or carry a sign for a cause, or to wear a shirt or give a speech, it is another to be committed to it financially. The question that has to be asked is what has been sacrificed?

So, before this is turned into a debate as to whether abortion should be legal or not, the question that has to be asked is, "What have you done, what have I done, to save the lives of unborn children?"

I am not going to give a speech as to why abortion

should be illegal but what I am going to ask is, "Are you willing to back up your beliefs?"

There really is no doubt but that the black community has been targeted. There really is no doubt but that the black community has suffered the most from illegal immigration.

So, my question is, "Do black lives really matter to you?"

I'm not asking you to say it. I'm not asking you to make a sign. I'm going to ask you if you really are committed to making a difference that will save the lives of black people.

Black women are simply amazing. They are smart and eloquent.

But they have been abused far too much.

Currently 75% of all black households are missing a father in the house.

A large number of black women are left to fend for themselves.

On top of this, our government funds an organization with millions of dollars that is used to target them and their babies.

Some women may flippantly have the lives of their unborn children ended; however, I believe most are making a painful decision and feel as though they have no other choice. They are often left alone with such a difficult decision.

Instead of fighting the fight to have abortions made illegal, can we not support these women?

Instead of giving millions to target them, why can we not give millions to support them?

Adoptions cost money. Can we make sure that every family wanting to adopt has the adoption funded? Can we care for and take in young black women during their pregnancy? Can we provide the emotional support for young women that are afraid, and confused and who have no where to turn?

Even if you are completely committed to abortions being legal, are you really against helping young women who have nowhere else to turn?

Please don't make this issue be about whether abortion should be legal or not. Please make it instead be about saving the lives of our black children. And let's not just talk about saving lives but sacrifice to save lives.

If we truly believe black lives matter, one way we can save literally millions of lives is to care for young, pregnant black women and see that their born babies are taken care of.

How sincere is our commitment?

I earlier targeted professional athletes. In the current environment there will soon be athletes who retire as billionaires. Indeed, with ten-year contracts approaching $500M, players who handle their money properly may quite possibly retire as billionaires.

Every year, the NBA makes approximately 30 new millionaires.

There are many black actors. Some are already billionaires.

I have no idea who gives and who doesn't. I'm sure most are very generous. Many, like Charles Barkley, a previous NBA star, are well-known for being generous. Russel Westbrook, a current NBA star, supports some tremendous literacy programs in Oklahoma. Warrick Dunn, a former NFL star running back, has built over 145 houses for single mothers.

With an organized plan, millions of black lives can be saved.

As I have said, the black community in the US has the equivalent of the eighteenth largest economy in the world.

The money is there. The influence is there.

A fund supported by professional athletes would draw many contributions from various sectors. Funds used to commit genocide given to organizations can, instead, be funneled to supporting young black mothers.

The biggest challenge to this is the many sell-outs in the black community who are eager to take such funds and use them for their personal agenda. The biggest challenge to this is the sell-outs who will in turn continue to abuse the black community while all the while destroying it.

This would need to be devoid of politicians and political agendas.

But before going forward, let me just stop and speak to those mothers who have had abortions and struggle because of it.

We are all sinners. We have all done things we regret.

As a matter of fact, if you are in that category, you can put down this book and not even read any further in this chapter.

What we do tomorrow is the only thing we can control. But please let's work together and mentor and support ladies who need someone who understands what they are going through. Let's truly love people together.

But saving black lives is not just a matter of stopping abortions. I hope that is clear. The government of the US has been involved in population control quite a while. The black community has suffered the most from this.

But let's see what can be done.

I believe in heaven. I believe heaven will be filled with children. I believe heaven will be filled with babies that were not born.

So, let's imagine being there. Let's imagine the sea of unborn black babies, 19 million to date. These are children that never got to take their first step. They were never able to wake up to presents on Christmas morning or blow out birthday candles. They never had a first day of school or pictures before a prom.

Look at the crowd. Was there another Martin Luther King in the 19 million? Was there another Barack Obama? How many Jim Browns or Michael Jordans were there?

Ok, there is only one Michael Jordan.

But what have we lost?

Because our government has poured hundreds of millions of dollars into funding an organization that blatantly targets black women, who has the world been cheated of?

How many elections would have ended differently? History has changed because those 19 million were not born. If nothing other than the number of votes there may be more black congressmen, congresswomen, and senators. The strength of numbers in the black community has been stolen.

What authors have been lost? What brilliant doctors have been taken? How would things be different financially?

Assuming that the black community is somewhere between the fifteenth and forty-fourth of 197 countries in size, how large would the black community's economy be if no children had been aborted?

To put that economy in perspective, at eighteenth, it is double that of Iran.

What would it be if not for those deaths? Could it be the tenth? the eighth?

So, when you ask or demand change, be smart.

What will produce the most change in the next 20 years? Is it promoting some cause that, even if you get what you want, will have very little impact; or will it be promoting something that makes the black community influential to the point of seeing many of the changes you want?

CHAPTER XI
It's not Race; It's Culture

They took the whole Cherokee Nation, put us on this reservation.
Took away our ways of life, the tomahawk and the bowie knife.
Took away our native tongue, and taught their English to our young.

Paul Revere &
The Raiders
"Indian Reservation"

Most people have heard of an Indian reservation. The reservations began because of the Indian Appropriations Act of 1887. There are 326 of them in the US. Every one of them is related to an Indian nation.

Not all of the 567 Indian nations have a reservation, however. When the US had won all confrontations with the American Indians, Native Americans were placed on reservations, mostly on unwanted and inferior land. There was little to work with. There was very little chance of succeeding on land that produced little in the way of good soil and wildlife.

What most people don't realize is the vastness of the Indian reservations in the US. The collective geographical area of all reservations is 56,200,000 square miles. That is about the size of Idaho. The largest reservation is about the size of West Virginia.

One of the things that make them unique is that they are technically countries within a country. Laws on tribal lands are different from the laws in areas surrounding them. For the most part, tribal councils have jurisdiction over the reservation, not the US government. They are "independent sovereigns", that were originally removed somewhat from the US constitution and its protection.

Of the more than 2.5 million Native Americans in the US, however, less than half of them live on a reservation.

One of the misconceptions concerning Native Americans is that their communities are low on crime and violence. They have not excelled on the reservations and rarely complain.

Though you do hear little complaints from them, like any distressed environments, crime is high. For the most part, compared to the rest of the country the quality of education is low, there are high levels of substance abuse, healthcare is often poor and teen pregnancy is high. Reservations are high in the concentration of poverty which breeds high crime rates.

Misuse of prescription drugs and marijuana by teens on reservations are about twice what the rest of the country is. Teenage pregnancy represents the third highest birth rate in the US with 59 of every 1,000 births. Native American women experience violence at approximately twice the rate of other groups. Violent crimes take place at 2.5 times the rate of the rest of the country.

Once again, these numbers are closely related to the poverty rate that exists on Indian reservations in the US.

These things do not often make the national news partly because of the sovereign nation status of an Indian reservation. Data is much more difficult to come by for those Native Americans not on a reservation; however, data we do have shows no indication that misery for this group any greater than it is for the rest of the country.

High crime rates, poor education, high substance abuse are not things peculiar to Native Americans. Instead, they are peculiar to Indian reservations and to poverty-stricken areas.

The Great Society was a set of domestic programs launched by President Lyndon Johnson. There were many good things that came from the Great Society, things such as the fact that many of the demands of the civil rights movement became law. A law was passed that disallowed job discrimination. Minorities were assured registration and voting. Housing discrimination was banned and, yes, constitutional protections were extended to Native Americans on reservations.

Between 1940 and 1970 the Second Great Migration took place. Approximately 5 million blacks moved from the South to the North and West. In major cities a similar form of a reservation was instituted for many in the black community. In 1964-1965, due in part to policies set in motion by LBJ's Great Society initiative and the War on Poverty, the black community was embedded into urban communities in a way that would change them forever.

I don't believe the Great Society was intended to hurt any race or community. Nevertheless, it did so in many ways.

First, let's examine how this came about. Many historians differentiate between The Great Migration, taking place between 1916 and 1970 and the Second Great Migration. Because of poor economic conditions, racial segregation, racial discrimination, and Jim Crow laws, millions of people in the black community moved from rural communities in the South to urban communities in the North.

In 1900, 5% of the black population in the South were living in urban communities. By 1960 close to half of the black population in the South were living in urban areas. In the decade between 1960 and 1970, 80% of the black population nationwide were living in cities.

The pull to the North was partially a result of the fact that there were jobs available. There was a shortage of labor in the north due to the different wars that took place. There were jobs available in the railroads, automotive industry, and steel mills. Northern companies offered free transportation and actually recruited blacks from the South. Job conditions were less favorable for blacks but, for some, it finally represented their first steady income. They were safer, though by no means completely safe. Their families were strong and would remain so until the 1960's tore their families apart.

The conditions and the lifestyle of the black population changed dramatically as they moved to urban areas in the North. Life went from that of living in the rural south to living in cities throughout the country. Culture changed. Lifestyles changed. Here are examples of large cities and how the percentage of blacks in these cites increased in less than a century from 1900 to 1990.

Los Angeles	2.1 %	to	14.0 %
San Francisco	0.5 %	to	10.9 %
Denver	2.9 %	to	12.8 %
DC	31.1%	to	65.8 %
Chicago	1.8 %	to	39.1 %
Baltimore	15.6%	to	59.2 %
Boston	2.1 %	to	59.2 %
Detroit	1.4 %	to	75.7 %
St Louis	6.2 %	to	47.5 %
Buffalo	0.5 %	to	30.7 %
New York	1.8 %	to	28.7 %
Cincinnati	4.4 %	to	37.9 %
Cleveland	1.6 %	to	46.6 %
Philadelphia	4.8 %	to	39.9 %
Pittsburg	5.3 %	to	25.8 %
Milwaukee	0.3 %	to	30.5 %

The 2010 Census shows further increases:

Detroit	82.7%
Baltimore	63.7%
Cleveland	53.3%
Philadelphia	42.0%

As time went by, the jobs that brought them to the urban areas would dry up. Many inner cities would become pockets of poverty. Housing units decayed. Just as Native American reservations provided few opportunities, so, too, inner cities failed to provide opportunities. As despair, frustration, and discouragement set in, just as on the Indian Reservations, crime became a problem.

Then, the final thing that would help tear down the communities happened. Through the programs of the sixties, many were helped. But two things would prove devastating. Many programs were only open to women with children and no man in the house. As jobs and opportunities dried up it became more advantageous for young women to participate in government programs without a husband. These programs ended up driving men out of the home.

Men didn't abandon their families. They were replaced by the government. The government was now the bread winner. They would provide housing, stamps for food, and a check each month. The government was now the protector. The police watched over communities to keep women and children safe.

A group who found their strength in family now had their families torn apart. In the sixties, 70% to 80% of families had a father living in the home. Today about 25% of black families have fathers at home. If you break that down to families living outside of the inner city and those living within, those living within our cities have approximately 90% of households without a man in the house.

The second thing that proved devastating to the black

community was the implementation of various housing programs. Public housing communities were built.

Actually, they weren't always built. Some were former military housing units which were built decades before. They were poorly constructed, to be used by soldiers, young men who put a cot in the corner. Now young women moved into them with their child or children. If you lived in a two-bedroom unit and wanted a three bedroom one, you had to have another child.

Section 8 housing was a step up. It would be better, but it was still limited to certain locations. Once you got into Section 8 housing, however, there was very little opportunity to get out. Even if you managed to get a job and afford to move, many neighborhoods would not allow black families in them.

So, the "reservations" were complete. Literally millions of people had moved from rural areas to urban areas. These communities provided little to no upward mobility. Fathers became mostly non-existent. Like every other community that is a pocket of poverty, despair brought crime. Drugs and alcohol became a way of life. Just like Native American reservations, the inner cities became rampant with high crime rates, poor education, and high substance abuse, the things peculiar to all poverty-stricken areas.

Without a job, dealing drugs was often the only income a young man had. Then there was violence. Killings on weekends became a way of life. Rarely did a weekend go buy that someone wasn't killed.

Of course, every person killed was someone's son or daughter, breeding even more despair. Gunshots were heard on a regular basis. Every young man had a rap sheet. Young boys had no father in the home, so they hung out with gangs. Being arrested was something that no longer elicited a shocking response. It was a way of life. Crime brought encounters with the police. It brought violent encounters as violent crimes do.

And then came the health clinics. They showed up at

every low-income community. But they weren't all just about health. In many such clinics, young ladies were targeted. By the millions young women walked in and left never the same, some forcibly sterilized.

Despair grew rampant. Poverty bred despair. Violent crime bred despair. Addictions bred despair. The loss of sons and daughters to gangs and to death bred despair. And finally, their unborn babies were taken away, producing perhaps the greatest despair of all.

What can we learn from this? There was a time when the government's goal was to stop crime. If the killings, drug use, and violence stopped; the people would be blessed. That is still true. It is absolutely true.

There are a lot of things to consider in addition to that, however. Of course, it could be that crime produces inner cities. But I think just the opposite is true. When people are born into places where every day is another day of discouragement and fear, crime follows.

Are black people violent and given to crime? Absolutely not. Outside of poverty-stricken areas, there is no proof that one race is more violent than any other.

Are people living in poverty-stricken areas with little hope of ever getting out given to crime? I believe so. I believe any group of people raised in the same communities would have been given to the same issues.

Are generations affected when, because of government programs, it is more advantageous to have a fatherless home? I believe so.

There is no reason for crime, especially not violent crime. It needs to stop and, until it does, things will not change. It is important to realize, however, what breeds it. If we are to make any progress in breaking the cycles that have kept person after person from succeeding, we need to stop focusing on the symptoms of the problems and deal with the roots.

Though it is a dauntingly huge task, though it is radical, the reservations need to be shut down.

CHAPTER XII
Here is Where the Road Divides

To this point, I have probably offended almost everyone evenly. I hope, however, that there have been enough things we can all agree on as well.

But now…

Any time one group dominates another, you will find people in the subordinate group who have traded loyalty and commitment for status, position, and wealth. Sometimes it is blatant. Sometimes it is covert.

Individuals are given special privileges. In turn for keeping the masses straight and under control these individuals are given special treatment. Depending on the times, it may be a position lacking in strenuous labor. It may be a position that is full of comforts or special food. Today, it is a position the person may not be qualified for. This position may give them notoriety, fame, and fortune. It allows a person who thinks an island will topple over if there are too many people on it to be given one of the most powerful positions in the world.

There are, of course, a lot of differences of opinion as to who is helping whom. I would just like you to consider several things.

1) If an individual fights for thousands and thousands of people to come to your neighborhood illegally to take your jobs, they are not for you. The people "for" you will fight for you. They will protect you. They will not change their stance for votes or anything else. They will not keep their cushy job while giving up yours. They will not first and foremost take food off your table and out of your children's mouths in an effort to promote another group especially fighting to allow them to break the law.

    Your jobs are important. Your livelihood is important. If you find yourself and your family without jobs while others have gotten the jobs you could have had, find out who is to blame. If people fought for groups other than yours to be in your neighborhood, realize they have sold you out while claiming to be your champion.

2) If someone fights for an organization that targets your people in a way that costs your family and friends the lives of their children, they are not for you. When someone appropriates millions and millions of dollars to a group that takes that money and makes it as convenient as possible for 19 million of your people's babies to be brutally murdered, these people are not looking out for your best interest. When they help fund a group who somehow manages to convince 13.7% of women in the US to abort 37% of all babies aborted, these people have sold you out while claiming to be your champion.

3) When a group of people passes laws that target your young men and take them away from their families, they are not for you. When these individuals take pride in the fact that they will fill prisons with your people, they are not fighting for you. When individuals construct a plan that will put more of your people than any others

in prison for life without committing a violent crime, they have sold you out while claiming to be your champion.

4) When a group of people push strict rules of conduct on everyone but you in an order to save the other peoples lives, these people have sold you out while claiming to be your champion.

5) When a group of people champions an organization that was founded on the basis of controlling the population of your people because they are feebleminded, these people have sold you out while claiming to be your champion.

This is how it works: Jesse Jackson has said the following:

What happens to the mind of a person, and the moral fabric of a nation, that accepts the aborting of the life of a baby without a pang of conscious? What kind of person, and what kind of society will we have 20 years hence if the life can be taken away so casually?

— 1973

Abortion is genocide.

— 1973

Those whom we could not get rid of in the rice patties of Vietnam we now propose to exterminate if necessary, eliminate if possible, in the OB wards and gynecology clinics of our urban hospitals. — 1971

[I]n the abortion debate, one of the crucial questions is when does life begin. Anything growing is living. Therefore human life begins when the sperm and egg join . . . and the pulsation of life takes place. From that point, life may be described differently (as an egg, embryo, fetus, baby, child, teen-ager, adult), but the essence is the same. — 1977

'Those advocates of taking life prior to birth do not call it killing or murder, they call it abortion. They further never talk about aborting a

baby because that would imply something human. Rather, they talk about aborting the fetus. Fetus sounds less than human and therefore can be justified.   *— 1977*

Some argue, suppose the woman does not want to have the baby. They say the very fact that she does not want the baby means that the psychological damage to the child is enough to abort the baby. I disagree. The solution to that problem is not to kill the innocent baby but to deal with her values and her attitude toward life -- that which has allowed her not to want the baby.   *— 1977*

If one accepts the position that life is private, and therefore you have the right to do with it as you please, one must also accept the conclusion of that logic. That was the premise of slavery. You could not protest the existence or treatment of slaves on the plantation because that was private and therefore outside your right to be concerned.   *— 1977*

In January 1977, Jackson wrote a 1,000-word essay for the National Right to Life News. It was one of his many statements on the issue, including an "Open Letter to Congress" in which "as a matter of conscience I must oppose the use of federal funds for a policy of killing infants."

He spoke at the 1977 March for Life and asked, "What happens…to the moral fabric of a nation that accepts the aborting of the life of a baby without a pang of conscience."

It was widely circulated by opponents of abortion because they were often unfairly portrayed as single-issue, right-wing fanatics. Here was Jackson, far left and multi-issue. The essay was written with clarity and succinctness.

In a speech to graduates of North Carolina A&T in 1964, Jesse Jackson encouraged the students to battle the odds as he had done. He told of being "born of a teen-age mother…a teen-age mother who never really had a chance."

As a Democrat running for president, however, Jackson reversed himself. He began supporting federal funding of abortion and has said that moral positions shouldn't be imposed on public policy. Freedom of choice must prevail.

"Women must have freedom of choice over what to do over their bodies."
Jesse Jackson 1988

Jesse Jackson of 1988 said that abortion is acceptable because "it is not right to impose private, religious and moral positions on public policy."

Don't agonize, Compromise

Have you ever wondered how a certain person obtained the power and position he has? How does an individual, who thinks an island that becomes overpopulated can sink, come to be named the eighteenth most effective Democrat in the 112th Congress out of 204 Democratic members?

How does someone who is voted "Worst Speaker" and "Most Clueless" by congressional staffers get assigned to:

> Subcommittee on Highways & Transit
> Subcommittee on Economic Development, Public Buildings and Emergency Management
> Committee on the Judiciary
> Subcommittee on Courts, Commercial and Administrative Law
> Subcommittee on Courts, Intellectual Property and the Internet -- Chair
> Subcommittee on Crime, Terrorism, and Homeland Security

Have you ever sat and listened to a person speak who was clueless, yet they rose to a level of authority, position, and power that boggles the mind? How is it that a person whose family had dismissed her due to her erratic behavior can move to the top of a political party being chosen to run as Vice-President? How does a person who has never run a convenience store or a lemonade stand end up with tens of thousands of people following her in awe as she explains how the finances of the country should be run?

It happens in all walks of life. Certain sports figures are picked over and over and over while better players are overlooked. Pastors draw thousands and tens of thousands only to find out they are completely lacking to hold the position.

It is simple. Sell yourself. Make a deal with "the devil." Throw away your convictions, your morals, and everything you have been taught and there will be people who need you to push their agenda and promote you to whatever position you want.

In the meantime, young ladies are neglected, babies are killed, both young and old go to jail for life. You, however, will live in luxury.

And, while you are doing that, accuse the ones who have, instead, stood for the hurting and abused people in your community of selling out. Who controls you?

There has never been a shortage of black leaders who are willing to sell us down the river if there is enough money and political power in it for them."

Stephen Borden Pastor
Fair Park Bible Fellowship Dallas

Powerful influential black leaders knew they had to be willing to look the other way to advance their political careers.

Charles Diggs

"In 1975 Jackson called for a constitutional ban of abortion. 'Abortion is genocide'. Yet when he realized he needed money and the influence of certain organization to support him to run for president he changed his views, The Democratic Party had sold out to Planned Parenthood and the eugenics movement. Jesse Jackson Went along to get along.

Stephen Borden Pastor
Fair Park Bible Fellowship Dallas, TX

The reality is that there are many people who will sell blacks down the river for enough money and power. There always have been. When it benefits them, there will be overwhelming support to secure our borders in part to protect the black community. When it has been decided, however, that a reversal on this position is needed to move your party ahead, blacks are once again led to the slaughter, with the full support of the black community.

Alveta King has attempted to bring the issue of black genocide to the NAACP three times. The NAACP has gotten into bed with the organization that brought black genocide to the black community. Miss King has asked them to deal with the issue or, at least, to discuss it.

In response, the NAACP has used buses to block demonstrations on the issue. Black paper has been put over windows so that attendees could not see the demonstrations taking place outside. The news media has hidden their trucks so that they didn't have to cover it.

Once again, power and prestige has taken precedence over the masses of hurting young black women and black babies who will never get to throw a baseball with their dad or do a cannonball off of a diving board.

The response from the leaders of the NAACP is: it will tear up the organization.

"Far too many men and women willing to sell out the community. Influential black leaders looked the other way in order to advance their own personal political agenda."

When you look at the number of African American leaders who have betrayed us over the years it is not always clear whether they are Uninformed or just out and out traitors. When we see pro-choice politicians defending abortion on television, do they really understand the implications of abortion and that it is used for black genocide?

Stephen Broden
Fair Bank Bible Fellowship, Dallas, TX

The NAACP and the media are conspiring to keep this information from the public.

Levon Yuille
Pastor The Bible Church
Ypsilanti, Michigan

"The Civil rights elite has forgotten the lives of unborn black children and has joined those who choose to kill them. Unbelievable! They have forgotten that in the past racists snatched black babies from their mother's arms and sold them in to slavery. Today they snatch them from their mother's womb and throw them in the garbage."

Ismael Hernandez
Executive Director African and Caribbean American
Center 2003

"Whether you are talking about the liberal social engineers who control the Democratic Party or the wealthy elites who control the Republican Party, or the media or the academic community, these people have created a kind of family planning cartel that does not tolerate descent. They have always been especially ruthless about this when it comes to African Americans."

Mark Crutcher
President Life Dynamics Inc.

Samuel Yette "The Issue of Black Survival in America"

"Samuel Yette paid a price that few others have the character or courage to pay."

Mark Crutcher
President Life Dynamics, Inc.

"...the American ruling class had made a hard decision, Americans of African descent would either accept their miserable lot or die...the venerable Saturday evening post issued a 'White Paper' in which it warned Black America that they had better understand and accept the

fact that absolute freedom and equality were not part of the game plan for them, and that the consequences of non acceptance would be wholesale genocide."

John Oliver Killens, 1982

The reaches of the betrayals know no bounds.

It is, of course, evident in the political realm, but it is evident in the sports world as well where organizations and media companies are desperate to promote their narrative. These organizations have worked for years to control the population of minorities and, especially, the black community.

So, they continue to find individuals willing to sell out their own people for fame and fortune. They continually put them in front of the camera. It doesn't matter if they have an education. It doesn't matter if the person is articulate or if they are in any way well read or knowledgeable in the area. What is important is that they are willing to do what they have been groomed to do and to viciously attack anyone with a different opinion.

Perhaps the saddest area in which this has occurred is in the religious community. From early on, in order to orchestrate a plan to limit the population of the black community or to completely wipe it out, the religious community was needed to play a part.

In the earlier days, ministers were given pre-packaged sermons on eugenics. Imagine that, pastors who have sermons constructed for them to convince their members the killing of their people was a good thing that would benefit them. It still continues today; many of our religious leaders have helped to convince their people that the murder of 19 million of their most vulnerable is what the Lord would want.

Unfortunately, there really is no shortage of individuals willing to sell out for power, money, and influence.

"The minister's work is also important and also he should be trained, perhaps by the Federation as to our ideals and the goal that we hope to reach. We do not want word to go out that we want to exterminated the Negro population and the minister is the man who can straighten out that idea if it ever occurs to any of their more rebellious members."

Margaret Sanger 1939

Notice how there is that attitude of keeping the black man in line. Use leaders that you give power and even luxury, too, to convince them that they have their best interest in mind while you continue to control their population. The ones that question, well, they are rebellious.

The *Religious Coalition for Abortion Rights* was originally created with the financial backing of John Rockefeller. They are now known as *The Religious Coalition for Reproductive Rights*.

There is plenty of money for anyone wanting to sell out their own. The United Nations Educational, Scientific Cultural Organization proposed that a commission be created by the US government with "a large budget for propaganda."

Years ago, there was a survey conducted. The question was, "Would you sleep with a complete stranger for $100.00?" Few said they would. Then it went to $1,000.00 and of course more people would. They continued up to $10,000.00, then to $100,000.00. Eventually, when they got to $1,000,000.00 virtually every person asked said they would sleep with a perfect stranger.

The interesting thing to think about is that, if you keep going higher, is there a point that everyone will do it? Virtually everyone would violate their own moral principles for $1,000,000.00. Some prostitutes cost $100 and others cost $10,000. Either way, they are prostitutes. So, with that in mind, I would just say that the question is not "how much do you cost?" The question is, are you for sale at all?

CHAPTER XIII
What They Said

You can go to any abortion clinic in America and see a steady stream of black women coming in and out. This genocide is happening under our very noses. About half of all black babies are now being aborted. In some cities there are more black babies being aborted than are being born.

Alveda King

We were told that birth control would reduce the number of abortions. Then they flood black neighborhoods with flyers. Afterwards abortion sky rocketed."

Cleaned Childress
Life Education and Resource Network
Northeast Director

Birth control and abortion are turning out to be the great eugenic advances of our time.

Frederick Osborn.
Founding member of the American Eugenics Society
1973

The best way to hate a nigger is to hate him before he is born.

Louisiana judge

Proponents …have argued this bill is for blacks and the poor who want abortions and can't afford one. This is the phoniest and most preposterous argument of all. Because I represent the inner-city where the majority of blacks and poor live and I challenge anyone here to show me a waiting line of either blacks or poor whites who are wanting an abortion.

Rep A. June Franklin - 1971

Early Civil Rights activists:

Those whom we could not get rid of in the rice patties of Vietnam we now propose to exterminate if necessary, eliminate if possible, in the OB wards and gynecology clinics of our urban hospitals.

Jesse Jackson - 1971

Black people are the target of birth control not because the ruling politicians like them and care about their economic equality, but because they hate them and can no longer use them in plantations and other cheap-labor conditions.

Muhammad Speaks
The Black Muslim Newspaper - 1970

I believe the entire question of abortions is just one more in the continuous series of events to eliminate the Black population.

Father George Clemons
Jet Magazine - 1973

The abortion law, hides behind the guise of helping women, when in reality it will attempt to destroy our people.

Brenda Highson. New York Chapter
Black Panther Party - 1970

The racists tells you to take birth control pills to kill, to murder life that might have existed if you had not. They are planning mass extermination of people they consider dispensable.

Van Keys Oakland chapter
Black Panther Party - 1969

A true revolutionary cares to the point that he is willing to put his life on the line to help the masses of poor and oppressed people. He would never think of killing his unborn child.

Detroit Chapter
Black Panther Party - 1970

Who the hell is getting the pill — the Mexican and the Negro. Do you want to wipe us out?

Cesar Chavez
Farm Labor Leader - 1967

Anyone who votes for Planned Parenthood programs in black neighborhoods is an Uncle Tom.

William Boone Haden

Into the black community stepped Planned Parenthood; only when they come into the black community they've become Planned Black Genocide.

William Booth Haden

William Booth Haden also said that free clinics constitute "genocide", a conscious conspiracy by whites to affect a kind of Hitlerian solution to the "black problem" in the US.

The idea, is to make less niggers so they won't have to build houses for them. If we keep producing, they will either have to kill us or grant us full citizenship. The Negros birth rate is the only weapon he has. When he reaches 21, he can vote. 1968.

Charles E. Greenlee

There has never been a shortage of black leaders who are willing to sell us down the river if there is enough money and political power in it for them.

Powerful influential black leaders knew they had to be willing to look the other way to advance their political careers.

Stephen Broden
Pastor Fair Park Bible Fellowship, Dallas, TX

What happens to the mind of a person, and the moral fabric of a nation, that accepts the aborting of the life of a baby without a pang of conscious? What kind of person, and what kind of society will we have 20 years hence if the life can be taken away so casually?

Jesse Jackson

Abortion is genocide.

Jesse Jackson

There are far too many men and women willing to sell out the community. Influential black leaders looked the other way in order to advance their own personal political agenda.

When you look at the number of African American leaders who have betrayed us over the years it is not always clear whether they are uninformed or just out and out traitors. When we see pro-choice politicians defending abortion on television, do they really understand the implications of abortion and that it is used for black genocide?

Stephen Broden.
Fair Bank Bible Fellowship
Dallas, TX

The NAACP and the media are conspiring top keep this information from the public.

Levon Yuille
Pastor The Bible Church
Ypsilanti, Michigan

The Civil rights elite has forgotten the lives of unborn black children and has joined those who choose to kill them. Unbelievable! They have forgotten that in the past racists snatched black babies from their mother's arms and sold them in to slavery. Today they snatch them form their mother's womb and throw them in the garbage.

Ismael Hernandez
Executive Director
African and Caribbean American Center - 2003

Whether you are talking about the liberal social engineers who control the Democratic Party or the wealthy elites who control the Republican Party, or the media or the academic community, these people have created a kind of family planning cartel that does not tolerate descent. They have always been especially ruthless about this when it comes to African Americans.

Mark Crutcher
President Life Dynamics Inc.

Samuel Yette paid a price that few others have the character or courage to pay.

Mark Crutcher
President Life Dynamics Inc.

…the American ruling class had made a hard decision, Americans of African descent would either accept their miserable lot or die…the venerable Saturday evening post issued a 'White Paper' in which it warned Black America that they had better understand and accept the fact that absolute freedom and equality were not part of the game plan for them, and that the consequences of non acceptance would be wholesale genocide.

John Oliver Killens
– TIOBSIA 1982

The minister's work is also important and also he should be trained, perhaps by the Federation as to our ideals and the goal that we hope to reach. We do not want word to go out that we want to exterminated the Negro population and the minister is the man's who can straighten out that idea if it ever occurs to any of their more rebellious members.
Margaret Sanger 1939

…we're talking really – and what John Rockefeller really realizes – look, the people in what we call our class control their populations. Sometimes they'll have a family of six, or seven, or eight, or nine, but it's exception.

Richard Nixon
White House Tape - April 3, 1972

People who don't control their families are people in — the people that shouldn't have kids.

Richard Nixon
White House Tape - April 3, 1972

What it all comes down to is we want the poor to stop breeding while we retain our freedom to have large families. It's strictly a class point of view.

Planned Parenthood board member.

There is ample evidence that government programs designed for poor black folks emphasize birth control and abortion availability, both measures obviously designed to limit the black population.

Dick Gregory - 1971

It takes little imagination to see that the unborn Black baby is the real object of many abortions.

Irma Clardy Craven.
Chairman Minneapolis Commission on human rights
and secretary of the Urban League

It was not until the mid-60's that blacks began to realize that what was called urban renewal was, in fact, what one black city planner labeled "Negro removal."

Roy Emiss
National Director of the Congress of Racial Equality
Ebony Mag - 1974

...less than $5 invested in population control is worth $100 invested in economic growth.

Lyndon Johnson - 1965

We looked into the family planning with some care and were amazed to discover that here is probably the single most cost-effective anti poverty measure. (In other words, abortion and birth control.)

Joseph Kershaw
Governments Office of Economic Opportunity - 1969

The government economic stimulus package should include a large increase in spending for population control. This would save the state and federal government the cost of having to pay for healthcare and education of poor children.
(100% approval rating from Planned Parenthood)

Nancy Pelosi - January 5, 2009

If you're going to curb population, it's extremely important not to have it done by the damn Yankees, but by the UN. Because, the thing is, then it's not considered genocide. If the US goes to the black man or the yellow man and says slow down your reproductive rate, we're immediately suspected of having ulterior motives to keep the white man dominant in the world. If you can send in a colorful UN force, you've got a much better leverage.

Alan Guttmacher.
Planned Parenthood and formerVice-President
of the American Eugenics Society - 1970

A majority of people in Colorado voted for abortion, I think a majority of people in Michigan are for abortion, I think in both cases, well, certainly in Michigan they will vote for it because they think that what's going to be aborted generally are the **little black bastards**.

Richard Nixon

… as I told you and we talked about it earlier, that a hell of a lot of people want to **control all the Negro bastards**.

Richard Nixon

… you know what we are talking about — population control.

Richard Nixon

Average negroes possess too little intellect, self-reliance, and self-control to make it possible for them to sustain the burden of any respectable form of civilization without a large measure of external guidance and support.

Francis Galton.
Cousin of Charles Darwin

The problem of the socially fit must be treated not as one of color but as a problem of the spread of feeble mindedness.

Dr. Davenport
Director of The Eugenics Record Office.
Co-founder American Eugenics Society 1913

We are paying for and even submitting to the dictates of an ever-increasing class of humans that never should have been born at all.

Margaret Sanger
The American Birth Control League

The laws of nature require the obliteration of the unfit and human life is valuable only when it is of use to the community or race.

Madison Grant
co-founder of *The American Eugenics Society*

The practice of birth control among the majority of colored people would probably be more eugenic than among their white counterparts. The dissemination of the information of birth control should have begun with this class other than the upper social and economic class.

Birth Control Review

In virtually every community where negroes dwell one finds them in fat times and lean alike contributing a disproportionate number to the rolls of the defendants and delinquents They make excessive demands on the white man's charity and over tax his patience.

Newell's Sims BCR
1932

The leader of the German nation, Adolf Hitler, has been able to construct a comprehensive racial policy of population development and improvement." "The difference between the Jew and the Arian is as insurmountable as that between black and white...Germany has set a pattern which other nations must follow.

Dr. Clarence Gordon Campbell
president of *The American Eugenics Research association NY*

Non-Whites are excluded from America.

Lothrop Stoddard
Director, *The American Birth Control League*

Commonly it is considered a great misfortune for America that Negro slaves were ever imported. The presence of Negro's in America today is usually considered a plight on the nation.

All white Americans agree that, if the Negro is to be eliminated, he must be eliminated slowly so as not to hurt any living individual Negros.

The only possible way of decreasing Negro populations is by means of controlling fertility.

Birth control facilities could be extended relatively more to Negroes than to whites. Since Negroes are more concentrated in lower income and education classes.

Gunner Myrdal

Gunner Myrdal was a man involved in Eugenics. Gunner thought blacks could not help themselves and no one could, so, we should get rid of them.

We will do it by force.

Donald Winkler
President, American Assoc. of Planned Parenthood
Physicians and BOD member - 1972

The world and almost our civilization for the next 25 years is going to depend upon a cheap, safe contraceptive to be used in poverty-stricken areas, slums, jungles, most ignorant people. Even this will not be sufficient. We need a national sterilization for certain types of our population who are being encouraged to breed and would die out if the government didn't feed them.

Margaret Sanger
founder *The American Birth Control League*

Three generations of imbeciles is enough.

Oliver Wendell Holmes

There has never been a shortage of black leaders who are willing to sell us down the river if there is enough money and political power in it for them.

Stephen Broden
Pastor Fair Park Bible Fellowship
Dallas, TX

Powerful, influential black leaders knew they had to be willing to look the other way to advance their political careers.

Charles Diggs

What happens to the mind of a person, and the moral fabric of a nation, that accepts the aborting of the live of a baby without a pang of conscious? What kind of person, and what kind of society will we have 20 years hence if the life can be taken away so casually?

Jesse Jackson

Far too many men and women willing to sell out the community. Influential black leaders looked the other way in order to advance their own personal political agenda.

When you look at the number of African American leaders who have betrayed us over the years it is not always clear whether they are Uninformed or just out and out traitors. When we see pro-choice politicians defending abortion on television, do they really understand the implications of abortion and that it is used for black genocide?

Stephen Broden
Fair Bank Bible Fellowship
Dallas, TX

The NAACP and the media are conspiring top keep this information from the public.

The Civil rights elite has forgotten the lives of unborn black children and has joined those who choose to kill them. Unbelievable! They have forgotten that in the past racists snatched black babies from their mother's arms and sold them in to slavery. Today they snatch them form their mother's womb and throw them in the garbage.

Levon Yuille
Pastor The Bible Church
Ypsilanti, Michigan

Whether you are talking about the liberal social engineers who control the Democratic Party or the wealthy elites who control the Republican Party, or the media or the academic community, these people have created a kind of family planning cartel that does not tolerate descent. They have always been especially ruthless about this when it comes to African Americans.

Mark Crutcher
President Life Dynamics Inc.

Samuel Yette "The Issue of Black Survival in America"

Samuel Yette paid a price that few others have the character or courage to pay.

Mark Crutcher
President Life Dynamics Inc.

...the American ruling class had made a hard decision, Americans of African descent would either accept their miserable lot or die...the venerable Saturday evening post issued a 'White Paper' in which it warned Black America that they had better understand and accept the fact that absolute freedom and equality were not part of the game plan for them, and that the consequences of non acceptance would be wholesale genocide.

John Oliver Killens - 1982

The minister's work is also important and also he should be trained, perhaps by the Federation, as to our ideals and the goal that we hope to reach. We do not want word to go out that we want to exterminate the Negro population, and the minister is the man's who can straighten out that idea if it ever occurs to any of their more rebellious members.

Margaret Sanger
1939

...we're talking really – and what John Rockefeller really realizes – look, the people in what we call our class control their populations. Sometimes they'll have a family of six, or seven, or eight, or nine, but it's exception.

Richard Nixon

People who don't control their families are people in – the people that shouldn't have kids. Now that's...

Richard Nixon

What it all comes down to is we want the poor to stop breeding while we retain our freedom to have large families. It's strictly a class point of view.

Planned Parenthood board member.

There is ample evidence that government programs designed for poor black folks emphasize birth control and abortion availability, both measures obviously designed to limit the black population.

Dick Gregory - 1971

It takes little imagination to see that the unborn Black baby is the real object of many abortions.

Irma Clardy Craven.
Chairman Minneapolis Commission on human rights
and secretary of the Urban League

It was not until the mid-60's that blacks began to realize that what was called urban renewal was, in fact, what one black city planner labeled "Negro removal."

Roy Emiss
National Director of the Congress of Racial Equality
Ebony Magazine - 1974

...less than $5 invested in population control is worth $100 invested in economic growth.

Lyndon Johnson - 1965

"We looked into the family planning with some care and were amazed to discover that here is probably the single most cost-effective anti poverty measure." (In other words: abortion and birth control.)

Joseph Kershaw
Government Office of Economic Opportunity - 1969

"The government economic stimulus package should include a large increase in spending for population control. This would save the state and federal government the cost of having to pay for healthcare and education of poor children.

Nancy Pelosi - January 5, 2009

The government no longer has to be directly involved in population control. That's why they have Planned Parenthood. At the same time, the government began backing away from the rhetoric as well as the actions involved with the issue of population control. As that went on, the amount of government funds contributed to Planned Parenthood increased by leaps and bounds.

In 1970, Planned Parenthood was the nineteenth largest health fund-raising agency in the US. By 2000, they were third behind the American Heart Association and the American Cancer Society, mostly from billions given by the government to locate the vast majority of their facilities in minority neighborhoods.

Charles E. Greenlee was once a staunch supporter of Planned Parenthood. He became upset that black neighborhoods had many clinics while whites had none.

Dr. Greenlee charged that the Planned Parenthood clinics, as operated in Pittsburgh, were devices which were used to keep Negro birthrate as low as possible.

"The Negro areas in Northside are saturated with three birth control clinics while the white neighborhoods have none."

Dr. Charles E. Greenlee

Greenlee also noted that literature from Planned Parenthood stated that, if women had more children, welfare payments would be cut off. In this they were lying to women.

CHAPTER XIV
So, What do We do Now?

Some people make their living by criticizing others. Sometimes, they are given TV shows just so they can spend an hour a day reiterating how a person or a group of people are doing things wrong. They point out mistakes. They bring guests on to point out mistakes. They themselves have little to no solutions but they sure know the ones doing the work are doing it wrong. Some campaigns are run simply on the notion that everything the incumbent has done has been wrong. It's embarrassing really.

So, I thought it only honorable that I make some suggestions. What can we do in the future to truly make changes needed? Who should be the beneficiary of these changes?

First, let's find out where the most need exists.

I love statistics. I think numbers and statistics can be a tremendous asset. Certainly they can be manipulated, twisted, and even lied about. There is a saying, "Let's take that statistic out back and beat it until it says what we want it to."

But where do we start? It's a big job. Some people say there is nothing to do. How can that be? Well, the challenge is the diversity in the black community. It is perhaps the most diverse group of any in our country. What I am about to suggest is by no means meant to be a comprehensive list. That is for someone a lot smarter than I am. This is merely meant to prove a point.

As I have mentioned, the black community represents the eighteenth largest economy in the world. They could survive without anyone else. Their economy is twice that of Iran. In a community that seems to be known at times for welfare, public housing, and yes, even crime, how can that be?

Well, there is a large group of black people that have taken good advantage of the opportunities in our country. They have studied hard. They have worked their way through school. They have become doctors, lawyers, professors, politicians, and businessmen. They have accumulated property, possessions, and businesses. Many have become wealthy, extremely wealthy. We will refer to them as Group A.

There is another group that has been successful. There are those who have done well in the arts. There are writers, movie producers, actors, comedians, singers and musicians. They have accumulated property, possessions, and businesses. Many have become wealthy, extremely wealthy. We will refer to them as Group B.

There is yet another group that has been successful. These are athletes. There are black athletes doing things and breaking records that people have only dreamed of. The majority of basketball players are black. The average salary is $7,000,000.00 per year.

Imagine that: making roughly $600,000.00 per month. The highest paid player makes over $40,000,000.00 per year. The top ten players range from $33,000,000.00 to over $40,000,000.00.

The average salary of an NFL player is $2,700,000.00 but there are so many more of them. The highest paid player makes $45,000,000.00 per year. The top ten salaries range from $29,500,000.00 to $45,000,000.00 per year.

MLB players make an average salary of $7,700,000.00 with the top ten ranging from $31,000,000.00 to $37,7000,000.00 per year. The highest paid black boxer in 2019 made $55,000,000.00. They have accumulated property, possessions, and businesses. They are wealthy, extremely wealthy. We will call them Group C

There are "pitch men and women". Michael Jordan has been paid $1,700,000,000.00 through endorsements. Tiger Woods has made $60,000,000.00. Kobe Bryant earned $323,000,000.00 in endorsements. This is Group D.

Denzel Washington is worth about $250,000,000.00. Dwayne Johnson is worth approximately $320,000,000.00. Oprah Winfrey is worth $2,500,000,000.00. In the US there are seven black billionaires, and the wealthiest black person in the world is Aliko Dangote, who is worth $25,000,000,000.00. The number of black billionaires will change radically in the next ten years as many of the highest paid athletes will soon be billionaires.

As I have said, the black community really needs nothing from anyone else. They could be their own successful country.

There is yet another group. The black middle class. The average wage earner over 15 in the US earns roughly $39,000.00 per year. From this, the average White person earns roughly $41,000.00 and the average black person earns roughly $29,000.00 per year. By way of contrast, Asians are the highest earning group at roughly $47,000.00 per year. The differences in income are mostly due to education and not race. Over 50% of black households earn between $25,000.00 and $100,000.00 as of the 2010 Census. This is group E.

Why is this important? It is important because it is simply wrong in attempting to identify a particular group to encourage to simply say, "black people". That tells us absolutely nothing. The black community is simply too diverse. The needs are too widespread. Some shouldn't be looking for help, they should be giving it.

One of the greatest actors to ever live is also one of the most intelligent men who has ever lived, Denzel Washington. As quoted prior, he said, "It's not race, it's culture." What does that mean?

Well, I had a conversation with a very good friend of mine one day who happens to be a very well-educated black man. He was raised in an upper middle-class family. He himself is upper middle class. As he began speaking to me of the plight of black people in the US, I asked him how he could possibly use the term "black people" in such a simple way. I challenged him that he really knew nothing of what others may deal with on a regular basis.

Slightly offended, he asked how I could possibly say that. I told him that he and I could sit and talk for hours yet, if there were a black individual who had grown up in a poverty-stricken community close by, my friend would barely be able to have a conversation with him. They would have absolutely nothing to talk about except the color of their skin.

Their journeys were radically different. Their places in life were different. Where they work is different, the communities they live are different. The places they shop are different. Their churches are different. The cars they drive and the houses they live in are different.

I suggested that, although the color of our skin is different, my friend has much, much more in common with me than he does with many other black people. I suggested he knows very little about many other black people in our society.

It is not about race; it is about culture.

This is important because it skews all of our data. There are those who like to use a statistic such as: 13% of the population commits 51% of violent crimes. That may be true if you want to beat that statistic until you get it to say what you want it to. But if we categorize individuals a little differently, we will see that it is more like 50% of violent crimes come from 2.6% of the population. If you take the middle class and above, as well as women and children out of the mix you will find a group of black men, living in poverty-stricken neighborhoods, who own these statistics.

Why does this matter? Because, when you isolate the black middle class, along with the women and children of poverty-stricken areas, you will find nothing unusual about the number of crimes had been committed in this group. You will not find an exorbitant amount of violence. You will not find a large number being killed by the police or even arrested. You will not find a significant larger number of traffic stops. The numbers are well within range of the rest of the US.

If you simply focus on black adults from the middle class and above, you will not see a great disparity in education or employment. For black individuals making millions of dollars a year to say they are afraid to go out of their homes is absurd. There are virtually no instances of them being "mown down in the streets."

The media and politicians have done a great job taking the lives of a certain group and convincing others that, because of the color of their skin, they somehow know what life is for those having grown up in poverty. One middle class Facebook person posted, "You have no idea what it is like to get killed for having a taillight out." He's right, but neither does he. Neither does anyone for that matter.

There is yet another group. Because these are ways I and I alone am categorizing people, I can make any group I want. We will identify them as Group F. This is a group targeted by a brilliant, brilliant man named Thomas Sowell. Sowell has been referenced by Coleman Hughes, another brilliant man. Sowell did work in the 1970's comparing certain attributes of black immigrant's children. He specifically focused on the children of parents first coming from the West Indies, Jamaica, Barbados, Cuba, Puerto Rico, etc. He compared them to children of black Americans living in the same cities.

There are things that are certainly different such as education, intelligence, culture, work ethic, etc. But there are constants that made it impossible to tell them apart. Standing them side by side you could not tell them apart. Because of this, both groups are subjected to whatever systemic racism may or may not exist.

What Thomas Sowell found was that the children of immigrants coming from the West Indies had an income of 58% more than the children of black Americans living in the same cities. Whatever one group was subjected to, the other one was as well. Nothing was held back from one that was not held back from the other. Any racism that one was exposed to, the other was as well.

Hughes goes on to talk about the Colombian Sociologist Van Tran who wrote an essay in which he compared these two groups living directly opposite of each other in the same city. They were equally segregated. They interacted with the same law-enforcement, which could not tell the difference between the two groups. They went to the same schools. They had the same healthcare. They were under the same rules and regulations as the other group.

The rate of high school graduation was much higher in the West Indies community than that in the American born community, however. The rate of college enrollment was much higher in the West Indies community. The rate of professional occupations was much higher. The crime rate in the West Indies community was much lower.

So perhaps Denzel Washington is correct. It is not race; it is culture.

Where then does that take us?

We have done a poor job because we have aided to create cultures that place certain groups at a disadvantage. This is not just about black people. It is about all of the subgroups in these communities. It is about Hispanics, whites, blacks, etc.

There is no excuse for violent crimes. There is no excuse for any crimes. There is no excuse for the fatherless homes and the abortions. It is true, however, that these individuals are less advantaged. They do not have the advantage of a father in the home to protect them and guide them. They do not have the advantage of living in a community where they don't constantly hear gunshots and sirens.

It is true that they have often made bad choices and that is their responsibility. However, WE have failed them. WE need to do better. WE are the many wealthy white and black millionaires in this country. WE are the black and white politicians. WE are rich athletes. WE are both predominantly black and white churches. WE are the so-called news media that would rather put someone down for their agenda than to speak the truth that would make changes. WE are the members of the black community that have sold out for fame and fortune.

What do we do?

I think it is relatively simple. I believe a group of individuals who really care about people can come up with a plan. It becomes complicated when politicians have their own agenda. It becomes difficult when one political party will not allow the next party to have a "win." It is difficult when hate becomes the desired response of the media because it provides a story.

What to do?

I am a Christian. I waited until now to mention it, not because I am, in a way, ashamed of it but because it will, no doubt, be used to destroy the message I am trying to give. I will be labeled and slandered. I hope the things I have said will be accepted before the criticism steals the message. I am a Christian. Because of this I believe any culture or group, whether race, age, or socio-economic status will do better following the rules of Christ Jesus. Because of this, I believe in the first of several efforts.

The Christian Community has to do better.

When people use the phrase "We have to do better", I

hope they truly mean "we" and not "you."

There are tremendous men and women of God who continually work in these communities. We need to support them.

Black and white churches alike need to pour resources into these communities. I believe this outreach primarily needs to be led by predominantly black churches with the support of predominantly white churches.

This is a cross-cultural mission field. It needs to be understood that our poverty-stricken communities are literally their own cultures. It may be true that, as a white man, I do not know what it is like to be a black man in America. But those black people living in non-violent and crime free neighborhoods are just as ignorant as to what it is to live poor in America as any white person who lives in a crime-free neighborhood.

I will say it again, it is a completely different culture that needs to be reached.

We need to provide big brothers and big sisters. We need to meet the needs of young women, pregnant and afraid. We need to flood these communities with men who stand as role models.

We need churches to plant new churches in these communities and not allow them to have to struggle each and every day trying to figure out how to pay their bills.

We need to put aside our differences and partner with those that have been in these communities for decades without our help. We need to continue to reach people around the world but realize we have a mission field here that we are neglecting.

We need to educate better.

There are programs now that need to be expanded. I'm sure there are hundreds. I particularly appreciate what Russel Westbrook of the Houston Rockets is doing in Oklahoma City. The following is taken directly from The Russell Westbrook Why Not? Foundation's website.

Teachers, parents, and students at Oklahoma City Public School's North Highland Elementary took part in The Russell Westbrook Why Not? Foundation's opening of the first Russell's Reading Room. Those in attendance also celebrated the launch of Russell's Reading Challenge, sponsored by SUBWAY.

According to statistics, the ratio of books to children in low-income neighborhoods is one book to every 300 children compared to one for 13 in middle-income areas. First announced in April 2014, Russell's Reading Room is a literacy initiative created to combat this very real issue and provide Oklahoma City children access to books in a safe environment where they can read with friends.

A formal ribbon cutting ceremony officially opened the first Russell's Reading Room at North Highland Elementary. Following the reveal, Westbrook, North Highland Elementary students, parents and faculty, as well as some members of the media, visited the room to see what great books were stocked on the shelves.

Westbrook has always stressed the importance of education and a safe learning environment, saying many times as part of his Why Not? Foundation mission: "I believe education is the simplest and most direct path towards a better life, so I want to not only motivate these kids to read and get involved in their education, but also to provide them with the tools necessary to successfully meet my challenge."

Russell's Reading Room in North Highland Elementary is filled with 1,200 books for children in grades Kindergarten – 5th Grade. Russell's Reading Room also houses a modular reading center, a stereo CD listening station and a listening library with fluency CDs.

Russell's Reading Room at North Highland is just the first of many, as Westbrook is projected to launch two more Russell's Reading Rooms within a year's time.

Russell's Reading Challenge is part of Scholastic's national Read 100,000 Challenge program that encourages students to read and log 100,000 minutes as part of a school team. Students can log their reading minutes online at the Scholastic READ 100,000 website.

To help get all the kids at North Highland Elementary reading, Russell and Scholastic gave every child a $5.00 Reading Certificate to use at the Scholastic Book Fair, ensuring that every child would own a book of their own and be able to experience the power and joy of reading.

Westbrook and his Why Not? Foundation has challenged over 75,000 students of the 147 metro Oklahoma City schools to read a combined 100,000 minutes. For students who read at least 20 minutes a day to achieve 2,500 minutes total, SUBWAY will provide coupons for, either a free six-inch sub to middle school students, or a free SUBWAY Kids Pak for elementary students.

SUBWAY will sponsor an end-of-the-year school-wide assembly for the school that logs the most minutes, with Russell in attendance

Jim Brown and Ray Lewis do things Brown has done for decades to support education.

According to Jim Brown's America-I-Can web site:

Amer-I-Can was founded in 1988 by NFL Hall of Fame recipient, Jim Brown. The program goal is to help enable individuals to meet their academic potential, to conform their behavior to acceptable society standards, and to improve the quality of their lives by equipping them with the critical life management skills to confidently and successfully contribute to society.

The training initially focuses on attitude modification designed to heighten the individual's self esteem and motivate them toward positive behavior. Trainees quickly develop an understanding between cause and effect relationship, behavior and outcome and learn how to make better choices.

"By experiencing small but repeated positive behaviors, the trainees are able to realize their goals can be achieved through multiplying individual successes. With a positive attitude and a desire to improve their quality of life, trainees are taught the techniques of life skills and learn to take responsibility for their lives and destination through self determination."

We believe that the failure in personal development and the lack of self-esteem are the root causes of the aforementioned problems that plague our society today. We believe that by enlarging the scope of individual lives, by introducing them to self-determination techniques, by motivating them with goals, by showing them how to improve and achieve success and financial stability, we will save lives that now seem to be lost.

The journey to successful completion of a goal represents the heart of the Amer-I-Can Program. It is the path and the understanding of each step along that path that is the backbone and structural foundation upon which our program solidly rests. Success is not only for the elite, well-educated, and the wealthy. Success is there for those who want it, plan for it, and take action to achieve it.

The Amer-I-Can Program will help participants develop their attitude from one of self-doubt to self-determination. We believe that in addition to understanding the goal-setting process, a person must honestly examine the whys and wherefores of past behavior patterns that have negatively affected their life.

"You can point it out," Brown said about protesting racial injustice on the football field, "but you don't necessarily want to disrespect the national anthem or the flag."

"There are outside entities that are trying to bring this country down," he went on. "We have to go back to the memories of 9/11. If that memory doesn't do anything to you as an American, then you're not really that sensitive a human being. When you think of the sacrifices our firefighters make, think about the service of soldiers in foreign lands and listen to their lives, you have to be careful that whatever you do, don't cast a shadow on what these great people do.

"They make sure you have the right so speak out without retaliation, or at least no retaliation other than other people criticizing you."

The full video of Brown's speech gives his take on protesting police shootings and the qualifications of well-known pro athletes such as Colin Kaepernick and NBA superstars LeBron James and Carmelo Anthony to effectively lead efforts to foster productive discussions.

"The bottom line is, it's easy to talk," Brown said. "It's easy to have the media to pick up on something, and it's hard to have the patience to put something in place that you can build upon that eventually will lead to each citizen having their equal rights."

In addition to efforts like Brown's, free tuition is a must, but it is not a must for everyone. Once again, we are being very narrow in our approach to reach the right people.

Free education is simple. Like most things it is made impossible by the government and the elite. I'm sure there are many plans, but here is one.

Who decided that a high school diploma takes 12 years? Fifty and Sixty years ago we had no computers. Today, we can have more access to learning than ever before. The high school education I received could easily be completed now in ten years. Who decided it was a 12 year program?

How many "worthless" classes do we need to offer? Finish in 10 years. Use the same classrooms and the same teachers to complete the first two years of college. Those two years would be a part of the current school budgets.

We could expand Vo-Tech. Every low-income community should have a Vo-Tech Center. After 10 years of high school, spend two years in Vo-Tech. Every current study shows there are currently jobs in the trades and there will be more in the future.

For those wanting a college degree, the third year should be an internship. One of my degrees is in Theology. Like most programs, the only bad thing about theology programs is that they are the wrong people, teaching the wrong thing to the wrong people, in the wrong settings. We fill the programs with academics who couldn't last a day in the real world. We take an 18-year-old who has never worked a 40-hour week and ask them to choose a profession they will do for the rest of their lives. After four years of studying things in a classroom, only half of which will ever help the person in their job, they start doing the job for the first time.

Our educational system is horribly out-dated. For the third year, go on an internship. The fourth year allows each person to choose the specialty in their field they are now equipped to choose. Those of certain income levels go free.

As simple as this is, the biggest hindrance is that colleges and universities are big businesses. To continue being such big businesses they need a bachelor's degree to be 126 hours, half of which are meaningless but important to their bottom line.

We need learning programs for younger children and a complete revamping of high school and college programs for our poverty-stricken areas.

We need to do better with housing.

I said earlier that we need to tear down the reservations. Many of our poverty-stricken communities are beyond repair. They breed discouragement and despair. They promote crime. They reek of fear.

An amazing man who has leveraged partnerships and worked with a multitude of other organizations is Warrick Dunn. Warrick Dunn Charities and Home for the Holidays are tremendous examples of what can be done when people and groups work together. Dunn was a star NFL running back. But he is much more than that and gets little notoriety for his good deeds. Warrick is the type of athlete we should be celebrating.

The following has been adapted from Snopes.com.

Warrick Dunn, who played 12 seasons in the NFL as a running back for the Tampa Bay Buccaneers and Atlanta Falcons, has been supporting single-parent families since his 1997 rookie season, when he started the Homes for the Holidays program to provide economically-disadvantaged single parents and their children with comprehensive programming for first-time homeownership.

Dunn's mother, Betty Dunn Smothers, was a police officer in Baton Rouge who was killed in 1993 while working a second job as a security guard:

Corporal Betty Smothers was shot and killed in an ambush attack while moonlighting as a security guard. Corporal Smothers was in uniform and driving a marked patrol car when she and the store manager went to a bank to make a night deposit. As they sat in the patrol car, three suspects approached and opened fire. They fatally wounded Corporal Smothers and injured the manager.

All three suspects were arrested after the incident and sentenced to death for Corporal Smothers' murder. Corporal Smothers had been employed with the Baton Rouge City Police Department for 14 years, and is survived by her two daughters and four sons.

Smothers' passing came just a few days before Dunn's 18th birthday and a month before he committed to playing college football at Florida State University (FSU). He was the eldest of Smothers' children, and by most accounts he assumed a father-figure role in the life of his five younger siblings.

Here's how the Los Angeles Times described Dunn and his siblings in a December 1994 article headlined "Turning His Grief to Good: Florida State Running Back Warrick Dunn Sets an Example for All":

Derek is doing well at Catholic High. Travis is fast and Bryson small, but he's growing. Summer and Samantha are running track and doing well in school. You listen to Warrick Dunn and hear a proud father talking of his children. And then you realize that Dunn is only 19. Still, he's in charge of his brothers and sisters, ages 11-17, now that Betty is gone. She was his best friend, a mother who worked two jobs, 16 hours a day, to keep the family together and to provide a few of the things that make being a kid a little more fun.

If there's anything harder than a teen-ager being asked to go to the hospital in a police car, identify his mother and then go home to tell his brothers and sisters what happened, he doesn't want to know about it. It was Dunn, handling things as he always had, the father figure, but now without a mother.

"I never really had a childhood," he says. "I've never been able to go out and just go crazy, like most kids, because I grew up staying in the house a lot, baby-sitting."

Dunn graduated from FSU and was selected in the first round of the 1997 NFL draft by the Tampa

Bay Buccaneers. The rookie running back was challenged by head coach Tony Dungy to give back to the community during his time in Florida, and so Dunn decided to start the "Homes for the Holidays" program in order to help provide homes to single-parent families in honor of his late mother.

The program managed to house three families during its first year. By 2018, that number had grown to 159:

"My rookie year in the NFL, in Tampa, I was challenged by coach [Tony] Dungy," Dunn said. He told us, 'If you are going to live in this community, you want to be a part of this community and give back.' From that challenge, I thought about my mom and her dream of home ownership, and that's how it all started. We did three homes in 1997, and now we're up to 159.

"I grew up in a situation where we needed a lot of support. I lost my mom at 18. Single mom, six kids, and a Baton Rouge police officer. She was gunned down by armed robbers at a bank. When she lost her life, the city of Baton Rouge started a fund for us. And that's how we were able to survive and pay bills. And when I saw that from the city, that really helped me understand what it means to care about your neighbor and to give back and support. I just think now I have been driven for so many years—this is part of who I am, to want to see people smile and help anyone that I can possibly help."

Dunn's non-profit, Warrick Dunn Charities, partners with other non-profits such as Habitat for Humanity to build homes for disadvantaged families:

Even in retirement, Dunn and his Warrick Dunn Charities are still partnering with Habitat for Humanity to build homes for disadvantaged families across the United States. At last count, Dunn and Habitat combined to build homes number 158 (in Detroit) and 159 (in Atlanta) and place two families in them before the holidays. Furnished, as Dunn like to say, "all the way down to the toothbrushes in the bathroom."

Dunn's charity provides a down payment for the home, completely furnishes it, and provides other services such as financial literacy program in order to assist single parents as they become first time homeowners:

Warrick Dunn Charities was created from the belief that a better future starts with hope. We are dedicated to strengthening and transforming communities by combating poverty, hunger and improving the quality of life for families and children. We help families thrive academically, socially, and economically.

Warrick Dunn Charities, a 501(c)(3) recognized nonprofit, has helped single parents and children thrive academically, socially and economically.

Warrick Dunn Charities has awarded millions in home furnishings, food and other donations to single-parent families and children across the nation to combat poverty, hunger and ensure families have comfortable surroundings and basic necessities to improve their quality of life.

Warrick Dunn Charities has furnished 182 houses in 22 different markets. They have served 495 dependents with 92% of the people served still living in their homes.

Through Homes for the Holidays there have been 180 families served and 488 children placed in safe environments. There has been $875,000.00 given in down payment assistance. Health and wellness support has been given to 250 families. Through their financial literacy workshops 468 people have been served.

Hearts for the community, yet another part of Warrick Dunn Charities has awarded $60,000 in scholarships.

We need to do better managing property.

Some things simply cannot be repaired. So much of our inner cities needs to be abandoned. It is not impossible at all to, over time, move people from these dark places. Though reparations are a bad idea and has no chance of ever working, there have been promises made that have been neglected. Many don't realize that former slaves were promised 40 acres of land. Though not completely accurate, the promise became known as "40 acres and a mule".

The following was taken from a brilliant man named Henry Louis Gates in his article, "The Truth Behind 40 Acres and a Mule" originally posted on "The Root".

We've all heard the story of the "40 acres and a mule" promise to former slaves. It's a staple of black history lessons, and it's the name of Spike Lee's film company. Such a policy would be radical in any country today: the federal government's massive confiscation of private property — some 400,000 acres — formerly owned by Confederate land owners, and its methodical redistribution to former black slaves.

What most of us haven't heard is that the idea really was generated by black leaders themselves.

Had the former slaves actually had access to the ownership of land, of property; if they had had a chance to be self-sufficient economically, to build, accrue and pass on wealth who knows how things may be different today? One of the principal promises of America was the possibility of average people being able to own land, and all that such ownership entailed. This promise was not to be realized for the overwhelming majority of the nation's former slaves, who numbered about 3.9 million.

What Exactly Was Promised?

It is commonly taught and believed that the policy of "40 acres and a mule" was a special field order by Union General William T. Sherman issued on Jan. 16, 1865. (There actually wasn't promised a mule in the order. This idea was the result of a discussion between Sherman and Secretary of War Edwin M. Stanton and 20 leaders of the black community in Savannah, Georgia.

Section one of the order states, "The islands from Charleston, south, the abandoned rice fields along the rivers for thirty miles back from the sea, and the country bordering the St. Johns river, Florida, are reserved and set apart for the settlement of the negroes now made free by the acts of war and the proclamation of the President of the United States."

These new communities would be governed

entirely by black people themselves. The settlements to be established would allow no white person whatever, unless military officers and soldiers detailed for duty, to reside. The governing of affairs were to be left to the former slaves themselves. The order stated, "By the laws of war, and orders of the President of the United States, the negro [sic] is free and must be dealt with as such."

The order went on to state three specifies the allocation of land: " … each family shall have a plot of not more than (40) acres of tillable ground, and when it borders on some water channel, with not more than 800 feet water front, in the possession of which land the military authorities will afford them protection, until such time as they can protect themselves, or until Congress shall regulate their title."

So this ordered 400,000 acres of land — "a strip of coastline stretching from Charleston, South Carolina, to the St. John's River in Florida, including Georgia's Sea Islands and the mainland thirty miles in from the coast," to be redistributed to the newly freed slaves.

There were a group of Republicans who were actively advocating land redistribution "to break the back of Southern slaveholders' power." So Sherman met with Stanton and the black ministers, "40 acres and a mule" was born.

When finally asked what 'they" wanted, former slaves, along with some who had been born free, wanted a quiet place to call their own, a place to feed their families, and to be left alone. But what

*was the main thing from all of this they wanted?
Land!*

*The chosen leader, a minister, named Reverend
Garrison Frazier, who had bought his own
freedom and that of his wife said this, "The way
we can best take care of ourselves, is to have land,
and turn it and till it by our own labor ... and
we can soon maintain ourselves and have
something to spare ... We want to be placed on
land until we are able to buy it and make it our
own." When asked next where the former slaves
would like to live, Brother Frazier said, "I would
prefer to live by ourselves, for there is a prejudice
against us in the South that will take years to get
over ... " Sherman then the order after President
Lincoln approved it.*

*A self-governing community with another
minister named Ulysses L. Houston as the
"black governor" was immediately established.
By that June, "40,000 freedmen had been settled
on 400,000 acres of 'Sherman Land.' " The
army was allowed to lend the new settlers mules;
hence the phrase, "40 acres and a mule."*

So, what happened to this visionary program? What
happened to this program that would have no doubt
changed the course American race relations? What
happened to this program that would have eventually
prevented the migrations of the black communities to the
North and to what would become our inner cities?

Andrew Johnson, a member of the Democratic Party
and Abraham Lincoln's successor, overturned the Order in
the fall of 1865, and, "returned the land along the South
Carolina, Georgia and Florida coasts to the planters who
had originally owned it." He returned the land to the people

who had declared war on the United States of America. The rest as they say, is history.

This was a revolutionary idea. It seemed impossible at face value. Is it so crazy to think this program, this order, could in a new form, be resurrected? Could we somehow, keep our promise after all?

The federal government of the United States of America owns 640 million acres of land. Our government owns approximately 28% of the 2.27 billion acres of land in the United States. States own approximately 9%, or approximately 204 million acres.

Giving monetary reparations will never happen. The numbers are astronomical. It would break our country. But a distribution of land, moving people out of the inner cities, therefore keeping our original promise and the promise of President Abraham Lincoln is not beyond the realm of possibilities. Then we just need Warrick Dunn to build everyone a house. Then we can shut down the reservations.

There are other possibilities as well. It may be a surprise to many to learn there are many towns for sale across America.

- Tiller, Oregon, has easy access to a national forest, stunning views of the South Umpqua River, and a larger-than-life view of the Cascade Range. This abandoned 256-acre Pacific Northwest town is for sale for $3.85 million.
- There is a beautiful community in North Carolina for sale which served as the location of Katniss Everdeen's home in "The Hunger Games" film franchise. This 72 acre town is for sale for $1.4 million.

Though it may sound strange, there are many communities in our country where there are houses and stores boarded up. At one time they thrived. For one reason or another people left.

What do these towns need to become reinvigorated? Often, jobs.

For all of the large companies in America trying to make a difference, sometimes it is a matter of putting the new manufacturing facility in a place with a lot of empty housing.

Granted, coming from an inner city to such a place may be beyond culture shock, but dream with me for the next generation growing up with parents employed and a place for kids to ride their bikes and play games.

We need to do better with employment.

There is nothing new and innovative that can be said. However, sometimes it is simply common sense, which there doesn't seem to be a lot of.

As far as suggestions, the first thing to do is to close our borders. We certainly want people from other countries to come here, some to make a better life, many because we benefit from them tremendously. To open our borders, however, and to allow literally millions of undocumented people to enter the country does and continues to do more harm to the black community and to legal immigrants than can possibly be explained.

Open borders is one of the true, utterly racist things we can do. It robs the opportunity from our minorities to provide for themselves. It is thoughtless and cruel to the many black people in our country in desperate need of jobs.

Once again, it is not as much of a problem for upper, upper middle class or middle class of black America. It is an assault, however, on poverty-stricken areas where jobs are a shortage and are needed so much. Please don't talk of the compassion lacking in not allowing people to come into our country by breaking our laws. Think of the compassion needed to help those in poverty-stricken areas to have opportunities.

The second common sense thing to provide employment is the opportunity to learn a trade.

I recently heard a story of a backhoe operator who had done work on one of his former teacher's properties. After doing the work, he said to the former teacher, "When I was a senior in high school, you told me I would make nothing of my life. You said I was going to do nothing more that dig ditches. What you didn't tell me is that I would be digging a ditch for you and charging you $75.00 an hour to do it."

Here are some jobs that need no four-year college degree:

1. Licensed Practical Nurse

    National average salary: $25.18 per hour

    Primary duties: Licensed practical nurses work under the direction of doctors and registered nurses. They take detailed notes to update patients' charts and inform their supervising doctor and nurse of any changes.

2. HVAC Technician

    National average salary: $23.25 an hour

    Primary duties: HVAC technicians install, repair and maintain heating, ventilation, refrigeration and air-conditioning systems. Technicians can perform all of these services or specialize in a type of service (e.g. installation) and type of system (e.g.

heating and air-conditioning). HVAC technicians can perform repairs on larger industrial units and smaller residential units.

3.   Home Inspector

National average salary: $52,066 per year

Primary duties: Home inspectors do a thorough inspection of the exterior and interior of a newly built or previously owned home to make sure it is safe to live in. They train to become familiar with heating, plumbing, electrical and structural systems in the home. They also need to be familiar with different construction methods and know the strengths and weaknesses of different types of homes. Home inspectors need to be physically fit to climb ladders and move through crawl space areas.

4.   Plumber

National average salary: $24.58 per hour

Primary duties: Plumbers install and repair water and gas supply lines. They also install appliances that connect to water supply lines, including bathtubs, sinks, toilets, dishwashers and washing machines. Plumbers need critical thinking to weigh the pros and cons of different solutions available. They also need to be physically strong to lift equipment and tools.

5. Electrician

National average salary: $24.83 per hour

Primary Duties: Electricians install and maintain electrical systems in homes, businesses and factories. On the job, electricians practice critical thinking skills when diagnosing problems. They often work with people and need good customer service skills. The job is physical and requires them to be on their feet and move around a lot.

6. Landscape Designer

National average salary: $54,862

Primary duties: Landscape designers work on outdoor residential or garden design projects. Their goal is to select plants and other features that suit the environment and beautify the outdoor space. Their designs change depending on the environment and may include vegetation, water features, pathways or sculptures. For example, landscape designers working in drier climates may use native plants, pebbles and rocks, while designers working in temperate climates may primarily use trees, shrubs and other plants.

7. Boilermaker

National average salary: $27.18 per hour

Primary duties: Boilermakers assemble and install boilers, tanks and vats that contain liquids or gases, such as oil and other various chemicals. They may also operate machines, such as robotic welders. Boilermakers' work is physically demanding, and they may work outside in a variety of weather conditions.

8. Respiratory Therapist

National average salary: $35.13 per hour

Primary duties: Respiratory therapists work with patients who have difficulty breathing. They assess and treat dysfunction of the lungs and provide patient care for all ages. They may also provide emergency care in cases of drowning, heart attack or shock.

9. Construction Manager

National average salary: $84,476 per year

Primary duties: Construction managers work with architects and engineers on residential, commercial or federal construction projects. The main responsibility of a construction manager is to assess what building materials will be necessary to complete a project and then secure the needed materials.

10. Dental Hygienist

National average salary: $38.10 an hour

Primary duties: Dental hygienists clean teeth and provide patients with preventative dental care. They also help educate patients on good oral hygiene, including how to properly brush and floss. The preventative care that dental hygienists provide can help patients from developing dental problems, such as cavities.

Forbes Magazine reports:

"America is facing an unprecedented skilled labor shortage. According to the Department of Labor, the US economy had 7.6 million unfilled jobs, but only 6.5 million people were looking for work as of January 2019 and it is more apparent than ever that our country is suffering because of it.
Take our infrastructure for instance. Roads, highways, bridges, locks, dams, harbors, water systems, and airports have been neglected or only marginally repaired in the last twenty years. Each year the cost to fix or replace the crumbling systems

soars, with estimates now in the multi trillions of dollars. And that's just to fix what's already there and falling apart.

The President has called for at least $1.5 trillion for infrastructure construction, fueled with government spending including public private partnerships and cutting red tape. Congress has appropriated some spending and promises to spend more. If they get this done, the impact on skilled labor jobs will be massive.

Aside from federal infrastructure spending, projected job growth in many building trades continues to be positive. The Bureau of Labor Statistics projects better than average employment in the building trades at least through 2026. The only problem is, there simply may not be enough workers to employ."

We need to provide our failing communities with as much access to learning various trades as we do access to Planned Parenthood clinics.

Reducing high school to 10 years and teaching a selection of trades in a two- year period, creates a perfect opportunity to provide hard working young men and women the opportunity to find gainful employment.

These skills could also provide individuals the potential to start their own businesses in their field one day. All of this for individuals who may have no desire or money for four years of college that often provides a diploma in a field already saturated with candidates.

Finally, this. As poverty-stricken communities begin coming to an end, many large companies need to be rewarded to locate their manufacturing facilities close to new areas designed to house those moving from the inner cities. Tax incentives, reduced prices in government owned property, etc.

We need to do better at mobilizing the private sector to confront the issues of poverty in a practical way.

CHAPTER XV
I Have a Dream: Unity

One of the most famous lines in one of the most famous speeches in history was this, "I have a dream." Well, I have a dream. I would love to be able to articulate my dreams the way Dr. King articulated his. I'm sure many will read my suggestions and claim they are impossible. Isn't that what dreams are: imagining the impossible and working to see it happen? I have a dream.

In my dream, we work together.

You don't have to agree with everything another person says in order to work with them and accomplish something. Way too often we see opposite sides as enemies. We get caught in the middle and we are the ones who suffer.

Career politicians seem to only be interested in getting more power or keeping what they have. In order to do that, it is important that they do everything possible to get us to hate the "other side". Lies are told, then retold. Good ideas from one group are shot down because the other group can't allow them to have a "win". Victories and successes are immediately followed by an event that is used to take the focus off of this very good accomplishment.

Recently, a group of Republicans and Democrats came together and constructed a plan they both agreed upon to help individual Americans through a tough time. Almost immediately, it was shut down by so called "leaders" because they needed the argument to continue. Solving the problem together did not serve their purposes.

We, in turn, continue to reward these people by allowing ourselves to be pawns to aid in the hate.

As I have said, I am a Christian. I am fully aware of the need some have to get you to think I am a nut. It serves their purpose.

One of the most fascinating events in the Bible is when Jesus prayed before he died. It is not the prayer in the garden but a prayer for His people knowing He was leaving the earth. There was one focus of His prayer: unity. He prayed that we would be one as He and the Father are one.

There are a lot of requests He could have made. He could have prayed for everyone everywhere to be healthy. He could have prayed that every need would always be met. He could have prayed for long lives for us all.

But, to paraphrase, He prayed the one thing that He knew was always to be a problem. He prayed we would all just somehow get along.

He knew that division and discord are the main enemies of accomplishment. He knew that even a great nation would grind to a halt in areas when hate and divisiveness was the order of the day. He knew that when people were to become more interested in themselves and their position and power, confusion would reign supreme.

And here we are. Is there a person that you can think of that just causes you to be angry at the mention of their name? Why? Often it is because it serves some powerful person for you to hate their adversary.

There is a wonderful story in the Bible of the Tower of Babel. People were getting together to "reach God." It was not a noble thing, even though it was an amazing goal and dream. The Lord looked down upon them and said. "If they can do this, there is nothing they can't do."

He knew stopping this was very easy. He changed all

their languages. The project came to a halt. Whatever the plan was, once the people could no longer communicate, once they could no longer talk things through and plan, the work ended.

And that is where our work ends.

When there is a phrase, or a statement, that causes communication to stop, dreams die. When people are so full of hate they will not even sit down and have a conversation and thus stopping all communication, progress stops.

Please hear this. Those individuals who are so full of arrogance and pride that they will not even have a conversation with another person are not only enemies of progress, but they completely sacrifice truly great things for their own agenda. Please reject these people at all costs. They are horrible leaders. They are not worth listening to.

I have already mentioned my admiration for NFL legends Jim Brown and Ray Lewis. Jim Brown is a man who lived through racism as a person and an athlete that few have faced to the same extent. He has long retired from the NFL and has become a social activist. From what I understand, he voted for President Obama and then for Hillary Clinton. As far as race relationships, dealing with the black community, and dealing with people in the inner city, he has no equal.

Instead of taking a childish view of refusing to speak with President Trump or to meet with him because he may not like him both Jim Brown and Ray Lewis showed their leadership and maturity by meeting at Trump Tower with the President. What was the outcome?

Jim Brown and Ray Lewis were among those who have visited Trump Towers to see President-Elect Donald Trump. Brown told reporters the meeting "couldn't have been better," adding, "The graciousness, the intelligence, the reception we got was fantastic." Lewis, said the meeting was about urban development and job creation through Brown's Amer-I-Can foundation. (Of which I am a financial supporter)

"What we believe with the Trump administration is, if we can combine these two powers, of coming together, forget black or white. Black or white is irrelevant," Lewis said. "The bottom line is job creation, economic development in these urban neighborhoods to change the whole scheme of what our kids see for our future."

Jim Brown has given advice for current athletes dealing with social issues. When asked if he voted for Trump, Brown replied, "No, I did not," then added, "I've been given respect. I've been listened to, and we definitely have a partnership." When asked how he felt about President Trump his reply was, "I fell in love with the man."

While others are pouting over who the president is, while others are refusing to even talk to him, while others are busy stirring up hate at the expense of finding common ground, great leaders such as Jim Brown are getting things done with someone it is almost certain he has disagreements with. By the way, this story came and went in a hurry while those lacking the maturity to even be polite are on the news over and over and over. Maybe they will learn.

I have a dream.

The first group that desperately needs to "change their ways" so to speak, is my group, those who are Christians.

We have let the world down. We have ignored standards within the Bible and adopted rules of right and wrong that suit our needs. We have failed to see that there are certain things we are simply not allowed to do. We have to stop rationalizing our behavior and live at the highest of standards. We claim to know better and then commit the sins that we should be ashamed of, and we are often proud of doing it.

There are sins of the heart and sins of the flesh. We often focus on the sins of the flesh and ignore sins in our hearts. Though neither are allowable, it has always been the sins of the heart that the Lord has found the most egregious.

To a woman caught in adultery who was sorry, hurting, and broken hearted He said, "Neither do I condemn you, go and don't do it again."

To the proud, arrogant, and non-repentant He said, "You serpents, you brood of vipers, how will you escape the sentence of hell?"

We look on the outside of people. It is the heart that exudes wickedness.

We have to have a higher standard.

Our standards may be mocked and laughed at, but we have set our standards way too low.

The Apostle Paul stood as a prisoner at one point when the people with him were told to slap him. Immediately, Paul responded by saying, "God will slap you, you whitewashed wall." Granted, it wasn't the type of trash talk that would catch on or that you will hear during a basketball game, but it was in the spur of the moment under much duress.

He was immediately informed he was talking to the high priest. At this point Paul backed down, explaining he did not know the man was the high priest. He responded with, **"It is written, you shall not speak evil of a ruler of your people."**

It is clear, we are forbidden to speak evil, mock, or ridicule our leaders. That standard is the Christian way. We have ignored it. We have aided in the affront on unity. We claim to know better.

David was a man after God's own heart. The odd thing is, for a man after God's own heart he sure had a lot of failings. He impregnated another man's wife and then actually ordered the man to the front of the fighting so he would be killed. Even when he killed Goliath, he cut off his head for everyone to see. Today, that would be a war crime.

How could this violent man be considered a man after God's own heart? There were several possibilities. Only once did he hide his own sin. However, I believe one of the things that made his heart right was he understood and respected authority.

Saul, the king of Israel, tried to unfairly kill David. David refused to touch him or hurt him in any way. He even punished the man who killed Saul asking him in surprise how it was he wasn't afraid to hurt God's anointed. David mourned the death of the man attempting to kill him. David was a man after God's own heart.

When a centurion came to Jesus to ask for healing for his servant, he first explained that he was a man under authority and in authority.

> *But the centurion said, "Lord, I am not worthy for You to come under my roof, but just say the word, and my servant will be healed. "For I also am a man under authority, with soldiers under me; and I say to this one, 'Go!' and he goes, and to another, 'Come!' and he comes, and to my slave, 'Do this!' and he does it." Now when Jesus heard this, He marveled and said to those who were following, "Truly I say to you, I have not found such great faith with anyone in Israel."*

In 1999 I was driving in my car listening to talk radio. A popular conservative talk show host was, of course, challenging many of President Clinton's ideas and policies. I was enjoying it.

Suddenly, he began playing a skit that mocked the president and his wife. I turned the station off and I have never once listened to this particular host again and I will not unless he changes his approach.

A couple of weeks later, I walked into a Christian bookstore and the first thing I saw was a large display of this person's newest book. He was, and I suppose still is, identified with Christians and Christianity.

Let me say again: as Christians we don't have the choice to mock, make fun of, or ridicule our leaders. It is an utter shame that so many people calling themselves Christians, some of whom are pastors, spend hours a day mocking, ridiculing, and assassinating the character of our president. It was wrong when it was done to President Obama and it is wrong when it is done now to President Trump.

When President Obama was in office, my children were relatively young. I was not a fan. However, we had rules in our house. No one was to speak evil of President Obama in any way. He was always to be referred to as "President Obama". The same approach was encouraged in our church with the utmost enthusiasm. The same thing applies today to President Trump. The same applies to teachers, police officers, etc.

The Bible says that rebellion is as the sin of witchcraft. People who would never even consider being a practicing witch, freely and gladly mock those in authority and those in leadership.

It is time we held our representatives to higher standards. Never, never, vote for a person who would mock a leader of our people. It is a death blow to our country. It is a death blow to our way of life. It is a cancer eating away at our youth. At the heart of it is often a desire and lust for the power of another.

Regardless of policies, our progress will be hindered by a lack of people working together. Unity will be destroyed by a lack of respect for leadership. Philosophies that excuse this sort of thing like, "He deserves no respect, we have to fight him, I am fighting for you," are rebellion, it is the show of ugly hearts, and it is done by people who know nothing about leadership and need to be removed just as soon as we can remove them.

I have made every attempt to avoid mentioning certain people but there is an event that needs to be addressed.

The speaker of the House of Representatives stood at the end of the president's State of the Union address and ripped in two the speech that the President of the United States of America had just given to Congress and the people of our country.

This is the man the country elected. That is the ultimate disrespect of authority. It is a public display of rebellion. It is as the sin of witchcraft. It is no different than having slapped our President in the face.

You may have loved it. You may hate him so badly that it caused you to cheer; however, it is wrong. It is a disgrace. No one like that should ever hold an office in this great land. It shows an attitude that has no desire to work together. It breeds attitudes in others who then feel the freedom to call him a clown.

It will breed the freedom to mock him. It will bring a curse on this country. It will bring an attitude of rebellion so that teachers will not be able to control classrooms. Crowds will come into the streets to burn down businesses and accost good Americans.

Once again, to the Christian community, black, white, red, or brown, we have made a commitment to follow the teachings of Christ and we are not allowed to speak evil or show evil to a ruler of our people. You may do it, but I promise, you are a big part of the problem if you do.

Now that I have addressed that topic, it is important to examine what we can do. We can certainly disagree. We are well within our rights to campaign against another person. We do not have to do everything we are told when that thing is in any way immoral. We should debate. We should make our opinions known. We are not puppets.

But it is time to get rid of politicians who do not have the maturity to respect others, respect a position, or respect authority. It is the epitome of immaturity and shows no leadership when a person has to keep the hate going long enough for him to win another election. It shows a bad heart and it is bad for our country and our future.

Don't let hate destroy us all. Dream for a time when the President and the Speaker of the House stand beside each other and explain how they have worked together for our country. Dream for a time when governors show respect for our President and work with him no matter what his political party. Picture a time when judges who have been a symbol of authority their whole lives are not battered by representatives from hearts of hatred. We really can see the lion lie down with the lamb. I have a dream.

DR. MARTIN LUTHER KING

1963

I am happy to join with you today in what will go down in history as the greatest demonstration for freedom in the history of our nation.

Five score years ago, a great American, in whose symbolic shadow we stand today, signed the Emancipation Proclamation. This momentous decree came as a great beacon light of hope to millions of Negro slaves who had been seared in the flames of withering injustice. It came as a joyous daybreak to end the long night of their captivity.

But one hundred years later, the Negro still is not free. One hundred years later, the life of the Negro is still sadly crippled by the manacles of segregation and the chains of discrimination. One hundred years later, the Negro lives on a lonely island of poverty in the midst of a vast ocean of material prosperity. One hundred years later, the Negro is still languished in the corners of American society and finds himself an exile in his own land. And so we've come here today to dramatize a shameful condition.

In a sense we've come to our nation's capital to cash a check. When the architects of our republic wrote the magnificent words of the Constitution and the Declaration of Independence, they were signing a promissory note to which every American was to fall heir. This note was a promise that all men, yes, black men as well as white men, would be guaranteed the "unalienable Rights" of "Life, Liberty and the pursuit of Happiness." It is obvious today that America has defaulted on this promissory note, insofar as her citizens of color are concerned. Instead of honoring this sacred obligation, America has given the Negro people a bad check, a check which has come back marked "insufficient funds."

But we refuse to believe that the bank of justice is bankrupt. We refuse to believe that there are insufficient funds in the great vaults of opportunity of this nation. And so, we've come to cash this check, a check that will give us upon demand the riches of freedom and the security of justice.

We have also come to this hallowed spot to remind America of the fierce urgency of Now. This is no time to engage in the luxury of cooling off or to take the tranquilizing drug of gradualism. Now is the time to make real the promises of democracy. Now is the time to rise from the dark and desolate valley of segregation to the sunlit path of racial justice. Now is the time to lift our nation from the quicksands of racial injustice to the solid rock of brotherhood. Now is the time to make justice a reality for all of God's children.

It would be fatal for the nation to overlook the urgency of the moment. This sweltering summer of the Negro's legitimate discontent will not pass until there is an invigorating autumn of freedom and equality. Nineteen sixty-three is not an end, but a beginning. And those who hope that the Negro needed to blow off steam and will now be content will have a rude awakening if the nation returns to business as usual. And there will be neither rest nor tranquility in America until the Negro is granted his citizenship rights. The whirlwinds of revolt will continue to shake the foundations of our nation until the bright day of justice emerges.

But there is something that I must say to my people, who stand on the warm threshold which leads into the palace of justice: In the process of gaining our rightful place, we must not be guilty of wrongful deeds. Let us not seek to satisfy our thirst for freedom by drinking from the cup of bitterness and hatred. We must forever conduct our struggle on the high plane of dignity and discipline. We must not allow our creative protest to degenerate into physical violence. Again and again, we must rise to the majestic heights of meeting physical force with soul force.

The marvelous new militancy which has engulfed the Negro community must not lead us to a distrust of all white people, for many of our white brothers, as evidenced by their presence here today, have come to realize that their destiny is tied up with our destiny. And they have come to realize that their freedom is inextricably bound to our freedom.

We cannot walk alone.

And as we walk, we must make the pledge that we shall always march ahead.

We cannot turn back.

There are those who are asking the devotees of civil rights, "When will you be satisfied?" We can never be satisfied as long as the Negro is the victim of the unspeakable horrors of police brutality. We can never be satisfied as long as our bodies, heavy with the fatigue of travel, cannot gain lodging in the motels of the highways and the hotels of the cities. **We cannot be satisfied as long as the negro's basic mobility is from a smaller ghetto to a larger one. We can never be satisfied as long as our children are stripped of their self-hood and robbed of their dignity by signs stating: "For Whites Only."** We cannot be satisfied as long as a Negro in Mississippi cannot vote and a Negro in New York believes he has nothing for which to vote. No, no, we are not satisfied, and we will not be satisfied until "justice rolls down like waters, and righteousness like a mighty stream."1

I am not unmindful that some of you have come here out of great trials and tribulations. Some of you have come fresh from narrow jail cells. And some of you have come from areas where your quest -- quest for freedom left you battered by the storms of persecution and staggered by the winds of police brutality. You have been the veterans of creative suffering. Continue to work with the faith that unearned suffering is redemptive. Go back to Mississippi, go back to Alabama, go back to South Carolina, go back to Georgia, go back to Louisiana, go back to the slums and ghettos of our northern cities, knowing that somehow this situation can and will be changed.

Let us not wallow in the valley of despair, I say to you today, my friends.

And so even though we face the difficulties of today and tomorrow, I still have a dream. It is a dream deeply rooted in the American dream.

I have a dream that one day this nation will rise up and live out the true meaning of its creed: "We hold these truths to be self-evident, that all men are created equal."

I have a dream that one day on the red hills of Georgia, the sons of former slaves and the sons of former slave owners will be able to sit down together at the table of brotherhood.

I have a dream that one day even the state of Mississippi, a state sweltering with the heat of injustice, sweltering with the heat of oppression, will be transformed into an oasis of freedom and justice.

I have a dream that my four little children will one day live in a nation where they will not be judged by the color of their skin but by the content of their character.

I have a dream today!

I have a dream that one day, down in Alabama, with its vicious racists, with its governor having his lips dripping with the words of "interposition" and "nullification" -- one day right there in Alabama little black boys and black girls will be able to join hands with little white boys and white girls as sisters and brothers.

I have a dream today!

I have a dream that one day every valley shall be exalted, and every hill and mountain shall be made low, the rough places will be made plain, and the crooked places will be made straight; "and the glory of the Lord shall be revealed and all flesh shall see it together."2

This is our hope, and this is the faith that I go back to the South with.

With this faith, we will be able to hew out of the mountain of despair a stone of hope. With this faith, we will be able to transform the jangling discords of our nation into a beautiful symphony of brotherhood. With this faith, we will be able to work together, to pray together, to struggle together, to go to jail together, to stand up for freedom together, knowing that we will be free one day.

And this will be the day -- this will be the day when all of God's children will be able to sing with new meaning:

My country 'tis of thee, sweet land of liberty, of thee I sing. Land where my fathers died, land of the Pilgrim's pride. From every mountainside, let freedom ring!

And if America is to be a great nation, this must become true.

And so let freedom ring from the prodigious hilltops of New Hampshire.

Let freedom ring from the mighty mountains of New York.

Let freedom ring from the heightening Alleghenies of Pennsylvania.

Let freedom ring from the snow-capped Rockies of Colorado.

Let freedom ring from the curvaceous slopes of California.

But not only that:

Let freedom ring from Stone Mountain of Georgia.

Let freedom ring from Lookout Mountain of Tennessee.

Let freedom ring from every hill and molehill of Mississippi.

From every mountainside, let freedom ring.

And when this happens, and when we allow freedom ring, when we let it ring from every village and every hamlet, from every state and every city, we will be able to speed up that day when all of God's children, black men and white men, Jews and Gentiles, Protestants and Catholics, will be able to join hands and sing in the words of the old Negro spiritual:

Free at last! Free at last!

Thank God Almighty, we are free at last

ABOUT THE AUTHOR

Todd Rawlings is from Keyser, West Virginia but makes his home in Chesapeake, Virginia. Todd has been a popular speaker and teacher for 40 years. He has traveled across this country and throughout the world, teaching as far away as India, China, and Europe. He holds undergraduate degrees in theology and education. He holds graduate degrees in theology and management. Todd has been a professor at Regent University in Virginia Beach for nine years. He has been married to his wife Rena for 26 years. He has four children, Alexis - 23, Ricky - 22, Bret - 21, and Logan - 19. Todd's other book, "Dealing with the Pain in our Lives" can be purchased on Amazon in the Kindle format.